D0227010

40 Days with
THE PILGRIM'S PROGRESS

To Be
A Pilgrim

PETER MORDEN
AND
RUTH BROOMHALL

Peter Morden has written biographies of Charles Spurgeon and John Bunyan, and was historical consultant for the award winning docudrama *C.H. Spurgeon: The People's Preacher*. Peter is Vice Principal and Tutor in Church History and Spirituality at Spurgeon's College, London, as well as a member of the Council of BMS World Mission. He is on the preaching team of his local Baptist church and regularly preaches and teaches at various churches in London and further afield.

 Ruth Broomhall is the great great niece of James Hudson Taylor and so grew up immersed in the stories of the great Christian pioneers. Her practical engagement with Bunyan began when she moved to Bedford in 1992 to commence her teaching career. Since then, Ruth has taught *The Pilgrim's Progress* in schools (recently writing *The Pilgrim's Progress: A Curriculum for Schools*), led youth and children's work at Bunyan Meeting, Bedford, and graduated from Spurgeon's College, London with an MA in Christian Faith and Practice.

Acknowledgements

Peter: I would like to thank Ruth Broomhall for being such a great writing partner and an important friend; staff and students of Spurgeon's College for stimulus and support; Philip Robinson, Tex McLeod and all at Streatham Baptist Church for providing a great spiritual home; Malcolm Turner, Crawford Telfer and Gary Wilkinson from the Christian Television Association for much encouragement; Sung Hee and Tim Keene for helping me to get published in Korean; Ian Randall for invaluable spiritual direction; Andrew and Lindsay Caplen, Naomi and Pete Dibdin for being special friends on the journey; my in-laws, Alan and Mary Vogt, for the way they welcomed me into their family from the beginning. And special thanks, as always, to my own wonderful Anne, Rachel and Joe.

Ruth: I would like to thank Peter Morden for the opportunity to share this journey; his wife Anne for her friendship, hospitality and encouragement; the community at Spurgeon's College for their warmth and welcome on my return visits in 2016; the ministry and fellowships of Bunyan Meeting (my spiritual home) and Providence Chapel, Bedford; and my family and friends for all their love and encouragement. A special 'thank you' goes to Sophie and Amy, my two gorgeous little nieces, who are a constant source of love, joy, hugs and inspiration.

We would both like to thank Rev Chris Damp (minister) and Nicola Sherhod (curator) from Bunyan Meeting and the John Bunyan Museum for their support and collaboration; all at CWR, especially Lynette Brooks, Director of Publishing, Katie Carter, our editor, and the design team.

This book is dedicated to our mothers, Pam Morden and Audrey Broomhall, and to the memory of our fathers, John Morden and Edwin Broomhall.

Copyright © 2016 Peter Morden and Ruth Broomhall

Published 2016 by CWR, Waverley Abbey House, Waverley Lane, Farnham, Surrey GU9 8EP, UK. Registered Charity No. 294387. Registered limited company No. 1990308.

The right of Peter Morden and Ruth Broomhall to be identified as the authors of this work has been asserted by them in accordance with the Copyright, Designs and Patents Act 1988, sections 77 and 78.

All rights reserved. No part of this publication may be reproduced, stored in a retrieval system, or transmitted, in any form or by any means, electronic, mechanical, photocopying, recording or otherwise, without the prior permission in writing of CWR.

For list of National Distributors visit www.cwr.org.uk/distributors

Unless otherwise indicated, all Scripture references are from the Holy Bible, New International Version® Anglicised, NIV® Copyright © 1979, 1984, 2011 by Biblica, Inc.® Used by permission. All rights reserved worldwide. Other translations are marked: J.B. Phillips: Scripture taken from The New Testament in Modern English by J.B. Phillips copyright © 1960, 1972 J. B. Phillips. Administered by The Archbishops' Council of the Church of England. Used by Permission. KJV: Scripture taken from the King James Version. Public Domain. NLT: Scripture taken from Holy Bible, New Living Translation, copyright © 1996, 2004, 2015 by Tyndale House Foundation. Used by permission of Tyndale House Publishers Inc., Carol Stream, Illinois 60188. All rights reserved.

Extracts from The Pilgrim's Progress by John Bunyan have been taken from the George Offor 1856 version. Public Domain.

Every effort has been made to ensure that this book contains the correct permissions and references, but if anything has been inadvertently overlooked, the publisher will be pleased to make the necessary arrangements at the first opportunity. Please contact the publisher directly.

Concept development, editing, design and production by CWR

Stained glass windows: Bunyan Meeting, Mill Street, Bedford, England. Images by David Stubbs, used by kind permission of the Minister and Trustees of Bunyan Meeting, Bedford. Visit www.bunyanmeeting.co.uk/museum

Cover image: David Stubbs

Printed in the UK by Linney Group

ISBN: 978-1-78259-586-1

Contents

Introduction

Over the next forty days we will take you on a spiritual journey through John Bunyan's world-famous allegory, *The Pilgrim's Progress*. Amazingly, it has never been out of print and holds its status as one of the top most published books in the world (behind the Bible and, more recently, the *Harry Potter* series!). Even so, comparatively few today have read the original version from cover to cover. Written nearly 350 years ago, it is a challenging read, in length, style and language. Our desire in writing *To be a Pilgrim* is to make Bunyan's inspirational and instructive story accessible to a much wider audience. We want to help you experience and appreciate the story as a whole while at the same time giving you a strong flavour of the real thing through a series of short daily extracts from the original text.

But why should we bother to read such an old book, even if it is famous? What is it that has made this book so universally popular? To begin with, *The Pilgrim's Progress* is a story that has stood the test of time, place and culture; a story that is relevant to each one of us because it is a story of the pilgrimage that we are all on – the journey of life.

Using a wealth of characters and symbolism, all representing persons or experiences we might encounter on our individual journeys, *The Pilgrim's Progress* acts as a great discussion tool for all ages on universal aspects of life, such as morality, behaviour, experience, belief and values. It really is a book for everyone!

Yet, *The Pilgrim's Progress* goes much deeper than that. It is, in essence, a spiritual story, an account of one pilgrim's journey from this life to the next. It is an allegory; all the characters, places, objects, encounters and experiences are symbolic in some way to the Christian life. The central pilgrim is called 'Christian' and as we enter into his story, we begin to understand what it truly means to be 'Christian' ourselves. Using his own experience, together with his extensive knowledge of the Bible and mature spiritual wisdom, Bunyan has created a unique and powerful account of the Christian journey from the 'City of Destruction' (a world without God) to the 'Celestial City' (heaven). Bunyan leaves no stone unturned in his desire, his passion, to convey Christian truth. His story guides, comforts, encourages and challenges us in equal measure. It draws us in and shows us how our 'Christian' journey can become an exciting, adventurous pilgrimage of faith.

The Pilgrim's Progress deals with a multitude of scriptural themes. Along the road to the Celestial City we discover the importance of the Bible, holiness, prayer, relationships, love and hope. We see the seriousness of sin and learn how to cope with the reality of suffering in our daily lives, but also we discover the source of true and lasting joy. Finally, we are directed to God's promises, to His faithfulness in bringing us through all sorts of trials to 'our safe arrival at the desired country'.

The passages we have selected highlight the key truths that were close to Bunyan's heart, the most important of which is grace – God's amazing, undeserved love for us. Bunyan's passion was for what he called 'awakening and converting work'. Bunyan was a great preacher but he was also a great writer. He desperately wanted people to know about Christ and to experience for themselves the wonderful freedom and amazing grace found in Jesus. He preached so that people could hear the gospel; he wrote in order that this good news could reach a much wider audience. It did. In writing what was to become a national and international treasure, Bunyan's legacy has proved a great one; much greater than he could have hoped or dreamed.

Wherever you are on your journey of life and faith, join us, experience Bunyan's amazing legacy for yourself, and be pointed to the God he served so well.

Peter Morden and Ruth Broomhall

Did you know *The Pilgrim's Progress* ...?

- Was written in prison and first published in 1678, a number of years after John Bunyan's release.

- Was controversial because it took profound spiritual truths and wove them into a richly imagined story, something innovative and greatly daring. Bunyan himself was at first unsure whether to publish it.

- Quickly sold out and new editions soon followed. Eleven editions were published in Bunyan's lifetime. The third edition was the first to use illustrations.

- Introduces the reader to over 100 different characters, all symbolic of people we might meet on our (particularly spiritual) journey through life.

- Has been used in funeral services of significant national figures, including: The Queen Mother; the Labour politician, Tony Benn; the British Prime Minister during World War II, Sir Winston Churchill; and the UK's first woman Prime Minister, Margaret Thatcher.

- Was described by the influential Baptist preacher, C.H. Spurgeon as 'the Bible in another shape'.

- Makes reference to 51 out of the 66 books of the Bible. The books Bunyan refers to most are Isaiah, Psalms, Matthew, Hebrews and Revelation.

John Bunyan's own 'desperate journey'

John Bunyan was christened as a new-born baby on 30 November 1628 at Elstow Parish Church, near Bedford. This was the local church that the Bunyan family would have attended regularly but probably more out of tradition than an active belief. As a teenager, Bunyan was strongly influenced by family circumstances. His mother and eldest sister died when he was only 15 and his father – a heavy drinker and swearer – remarried soon after. To escape what was for him a deeply unhappy home life, he enlisted for the Parliamentary army in the terrible English Civil War. He later records how on at least one occasion he was delivered from death.

By 1649 he was back home in Elstow and trading as a 'tinker', a simple maker and mender of pots and pans. He married his first wife (thought to be named Mary). She came from a godly home and brought with her two Christian books, which had belonged to her father. Inspired by them, Bunyan started attending Elstow Parish Church during the week as well as on Sundays. So began a period of intense spiritual struggles for Bunyan, vividly described in his spiritual autobiography *Grace Abounding to the Chief of Sinners*. While Bunyan as yet had no personal understanding or experience of 'grace', conviction of his sinfulness before God grew stronger and so his own 'great burden' grew heavier.

Then one day he overheard a few impoverished women in Bedford talking about God, a new birth and the work of God in their hearts. He noticed that they had a certain joy as they spoke. This was an experience as yet unknown to Bunyan. He became a member of their church, a small independent congregation in Bedford, which was led by John Gifford, Bunyan's first true spiritual guide and the inspiration for the character 'Evangelist' in *The Pilgrim's Progress*. Through him, Bunyan came to know Christ as his Saviour. This was the major turning point in Bunyan's life. From then on he was devoted to God.

Bunyan's own Christian journey was to prove a difficult one. During a lifetime of Christian service to God as a pastor, preacher and writer, Bunyan endured much pain and trouble. His eldest child was born blind and another stillborn, his first wife died at a young age, leaving him with four young children to look after, and he endured two terms in prison, the first of which lasted twelve years.

He died in 1688, having caught a fever after getting soaked through on a journey to London. By this stage he was already well known. Following his death his fame spread and by the nineteenth century he was being praised as one of the greatest ever Englishmen. The impoverished tinker from Elstow had become a national celebrity. But fame would have meant nothing to Bunyan, except for its role in 'awakening and converting work'. This was his heart, his passion. This is what inspired him to write his greatest and most memorable work, *The Pilgrim's Progress*.

How to use this book

Using the story as a guide, each of the forty days is given a theme and a related Bible reading or readings. There is a short introductory section, which helps tell the unfolding story of *The Pilgrim's Progress* and provides the links between the chosen passages from the book. Following this is an extract from *The Pilgrim's Progress,* followed by a reflection. Each day ends with an idea or ideas for you to 'ponder' and a short written prayer for you to use.

It may well be you take longer than forty days to work through the readings and reflections. If so, don't worry. In fact, if you are really struck by a reading, or a thought, you might want to pause and return to it the next day as well. And if you find you go a few days without reading, don't give up. The days are designed so that you can easily pick up from the day before. We believe working through these reflections is a journey in itself, one that needn't be rushed. You may find you get the most from the readings and reflections if you keep a notebook or a journal handy, so you can record your own thoughts and prayers. So, take the time that you need: meditate, reflect, pray. Travelling the journey in God's good timing, one step at a time, is the main thing.

One further word about Bunyan's writing. As we noted before, many have found it 'challenging'. This is not surprising. Language has changed much since the seventeenth century, but don't be put off. Bunyan's own writing is, like Shakespeare's, extraordinarily powerful, with great strength and rhythm, full of memorable phrases and arresting imagery. So we have kept as closely to the original as we felt we could, preserving the 'thees' and 'thous' and the vast majority of the original language, only very occasionally adding alternatives where the meaning might be unclear, or where, perhaps, the word Bunyan used has come to mean something else today. So, as you read the extracts, be assured you're really reading Bunyan! If there's a word or idea you don't understand, or if you find it difficult, we hope the reflections we have written will make things clearer.

Yes, Bunyan's writing is 'strong meat', but it will take us deeper. The lessons learned have the potential to be truly transformative.

The light

THE WRATH TO COME

To the glory of god and in commemoration of the ter-centenary of bunyan meeting (1650–1950) Evangelist (John Gifford, Minister 1650–55) points the way to Christian (John Bunyan, Minister 1671–88)

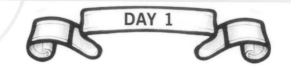

A burden too heavy to bear

Psalm 38:4,21–22

Welcome to the start of our journey through *The Pilgrim's Progress*! It opens with a famous passage, in which Bunyan takes the role of the narrator or 'dreamer'. The passage introduces us to the central character of the story, a pilgrim who Bunyan simply calls 'Christian'. He is symbolic of all men and women who respond to God's call to set off on their own journey of faith and discipleship. The story is inspired, in part at least, by Bunyan's own experience of the adventure that is the Christian life. He almost certainly wrote *The Pilgrim's Progress* towards the end of his twelve years in Bedford county jail. The 'den' he refers to here is his dark and dingy prison cell.

As I walked through the wilderness of this world, I lighted on a certain place, where was a den; and I laid me down in that place to sleep: and as I slept, I dreamed a dream. I dreamed, and, behold, I saw a man clothed with rags, standing in a certain place, with his face from his own house, a book in his hand, and a great burden upon his back. I looked, and saw him open the book, and read therein; and as he read, he wept and trembled; and not being able longer to contain, he brake out with a lamentable cry, saying, What shall I do?

An overarching theme of *The Pilgrim's Progress* is that we are deeply loved by God, more loved than we could ever imagine. Does that sound good? If so, read on! This great book has a huge amount to say about the amazing love of God, which flows out to each one of us.

But that is not where the story begins. Rather, it starts with what may seem a surprising theme. It starts with sin. In Bunyan's dream, he sees a man with a great burden strapped tightly to his back. This great and terrible burden is one of Bunyan's best known images. It represents the crushing weight of sin that Bunyan's pilgrim carries round with him. It is an image that resonates with the Bible's own language, for the psalmist in Psalm 38 speaks of his guilt as 'a burden too heavy to bear' (v4). Bunyan wants us to understand that everyone has this burden.

What is sin? It is more than the wrong things we do, although it certainly does include this. It is our rebellion against God. It's when we put ourselves first, and live our lives without reference to God. Such sin is serious, deadly serious in fact. For it separates us from God.

Down the ages, those who have truly understood this have often stood with Bunyan's pilgrim, shaken and weeping. Does it seem strange to hear these things? If so, it may be because, in our twenty-first century culture, we seldom speak of sin. Even in some churches, it's almost a taboo subject. But the twenty-first century world is getting it wrong when it dismisses sin and says it's an outmoded idea. As our Bible readings today show us, sin is real, sin is serious, and sin needs to be dealt with.

But the wonderful news is that, in Jesus, there is hope! The 'book' that the trembling pilgrim holds in his hands is none other than the Bible. It has highlighted the reality and the awful consequences of sin. But it also points the way to Jesus.

God loves us in spite of our sin and rebellion, and so He sent His Son Jesus to take the punishment for all humankind's sin. Jesus died on the cross – a once and for all sacrifice. But that wasn't the end. When Jesus rose to life again, His victory was also ours. The burden of sin can now be lifted and we are no longer separated from God. When we realise this, it makes God's love all the more wonderful. As American pastor Timothy Keller has put it, 'We are more sinful and flawed in ourselves than we ever dared believe, yet at the very same time we are more loved and accepted in Jesus Christ than we ever dared hope.'* This is the heart of the 'good news' of Jesus.

TO PONDER …

Perhaps you are reading this and you realise your burden of sin has never been dealt with. Turn from your sin and turn to Jesus, trusting Him as your own personal Saviour and Lord. When you place your trust in Christ, you will begin your own adventurous journey – a journey you will discover lots more about over the next forty days.

PRAYER

Father God, thank You that You love me more than I ever dared hope, even though I'm more sinful than I ever realised. Thank You for sending Your Son, Jesus, to die and rise again for me. Because of what He did, You offer me forgiveness. I turn from my sin and turn to You. Thank You, Jesus, for being my personal Saviour and my Lord. Amen.

˟Timothy Keller, *The Meaning of Marriage* (London: Hodder & Stoughton, 2011)

Jesus – light of the world

John 8:12; 2 Peter 1:19

As the pilgrim (Christian) continues to read his book – the Bible – he becomes more and more distressed. At first he tries to hide this distress from his wife and children, but then he begins to talk to them about his burden and his fears that their city 'will be burned with fire from heaven'. His family thinks he is ill and sends him to bed, hoping that he will be better by morning. But Christian cannot sleep and becomes increasingly troubled, while his family becomes less and less sympathetic. Some days later, he sees a man, called Evangelist, coming towards him. Evangelist asks what is wrong. Christian tells him of his burden and of his fears of 'the grave', hell and 'judgment'.

Evangelist listens to Christian's cries and responds with further questions before pointing him in the right direction.

> Then said Evangelist, If this be thy condition, why standest thou still? He answered, Because I know not whither to go. Then he gave him a parchment roll, and there was written within, 'Fly from the wrath to come'.

> The man therefore, read it, and looking upon Evangelist very carefully, said, Whither must I fly? Then said Evangelist, pointing with his finger over a very wide field, Do you see yonder wicket gate? The man said, No. Then said the other, Do you see yonder shining light? He said, I think I do. Then said Evangelist, Keep that light in your eye, and go up directly thereto, so shalt thou see the gate; at which, when thou knockest, it shall be told thee what thou shalt do.

So I saw in my dream that the man began to run. Now he had not run far from his own door, but his wife and children perceiving it, began to cry after him to return; but the man put his fingers in his ears, and ran on, crying, Life! life! Eternal life. So he looked not behind him, but fled towards the middle of the plain.

Bunyan's pilgrim continues to feel deep distress. He has this terrible burden of sin and rightly fears the judgment to come. What's more, he simply does not know what to do. There seems to be no way of escape. He is in darkness.

Then the wonderful character of Evangelist enters the story. What he does is actually quite simple. He points Christian towards the light. Once directed, Christian needs no further invitation. He doesn't just walk towards the light, he runs. Where the light is there is a gate, symbolising conversion: the point at which he becomes a Christian. It is here he will find Jesus, the 'light of the world' (John 8:12). No wonder he runs.

Who is it who pointed you – or *is* pointing you – to the light? Perhaps one of your parents, or both of them? Maybe a brother, or sister, or friend, or someone you hardly knew or know? Probably you can think of more than one person, but often someone was especially influential. The person who pointed Bunyan to Christ was John Gifford, his pastor, who was almost certainly the model for the character of Evangelist. Gifford was a very different type of man to Bunyan. In the English Civil War they had been on opposite sides: Gifford had been a 'Royalist' officer, Bunyan a lowly 'Parliamentary' private. It's fair to say the two would not have been natural friends! But after the war, Gifford himself experienced conversion and became a changed man. He lived for Christ and loved to share the gospel message with others. He was more than willing to reach out to someone like Bunyan. Praise God for people like John Gifford.

Is there a 'John Gifford' in your own story? If someone pointed you to Jesus and you are still in close touch with them, thank them personally for what they did, even if you've said before how grateful you are. If it was someone you're not now in touch with, and they're still alive, why not try and find some contact details and drop them a line to thank them? Most likely this will be hugely appreciated! Even if this is not possible, you can still thank God for them, and for what they did.

And there is a vital question here too. Who is it that God is calling you to point towards the light? Although not all Christians are called to be evangelists, every follower of Jesus is called to be a witness, a light shining in a darkened world, reflecting the one true light of the world, the Saviour, Jesus Christ. There is a mistaken way to do this: we can be hard, abrasive and judgmental of others. But Bunyan's Evangelist shows us a better way: he simply points the unhappy pilgrim to Jesus. We can do this through loving others, listening and caring. If we live as 'children of light' that is a great witness. But we also need to speak, as God gives us opportunities, directing people to Jesus who has done so much for us. To reflect Christ's light is to live and to speak for Christ.

TO PONDER …

Write down the names of three people you would like to share more of your faith with. Pray for these people, and ask God for opportunities to share the gospel not only through what you say but by how you live.

PRAYER

Father, I praise You for Jesus, the light of the world, and thank You for those who pointed me to Him. Help me to point others to Jesus. I lift before You these three people. Help me to listen, to care and to love them. And help me, as You give me opportunity, to speak about Jesus. I pray for my friends that, like Bunyan's pilgrim, they too would come to know Christ personally. Amen.

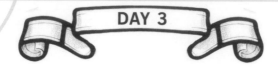

Saved by grace

Galatians 3:10–14; Hebrews 2:3

Christian's neighbours see him running towards the light and try, through various means, to get him to return. Two of them, Obstinate and Pliable, resolve 'to fetch him back by force' but he pleads with them to join him. Living up to their names, Obstinate refuses while Pliable is persuaded. Christian and Pliable continue on together, but difficulty confronts them when they stumble into the Slough of Despond, a miry bog, symbolic of sin and despair. Pliable quickly gives up and returns home. Christian, struggling with the heavy burden on his back, eventually manages to get out of the Slough thanks to a man aptly named Help. Safely through, Christian continues on his way, still carrying his burden.

Christian's next encounter is with a man named Mr Worldly-wiseman. This man symbolises the world's belief that morality and good works will overcome sin, a belief that will inevitably fail. At this point, Christian has not yet encountered Christ and does not know about true saving grace – he has not yet truly become a Christian. So mistakenly he concludes that Mr Worldly-wiseman is worth listening to and asks for directions.

CHRISTIAN: *Sir, which is my way to this honest man's house?*

MR. WORLDLY-WISEMAN: *Do you see yonder hill?*

CHRISTIAN: *Yes, very well.*

MR. WORLDLY-WISEMAN: *By that hill you must go, and the first house you come at is his.*

So Christian turned out of his way, to go to Mr. Legality's house for help; but, behold, when he was got now hard by the hill, it seemed so high, and also that side of it that was next the way-side, did hang so much over, that Christian was afraid to venture further, lest the hill should fall on his head; wherefore there he stood still, and wotted [knew] not what to do. Also his burden now seemed heavier to him, than while he was in his way. There came also flashes of fire out of the hill, that made Christian afraid that he should be burned. Here, therefore, he sweat and did quake for fear. And now he began to be sorry that he had taken Mr. Worldly-wiseman's counsel. And with that he saw Evangelist coming to meet him; at the sight also of whom he began to blush for shame.

We cannot save ourselves. Worldly-wiseman and Legality represent all such attempts, and they are doomed to failure. If we try, the hill is far too high and the burden only gets bigger and heavier with each advancing step. As weary Christian tries to work his way to God, he becomes so dispirited and afraid he thinks the terrible, toilsome hill might just fall on his head. It's an image that was particularly vivid for Bunyan. As a young man, he used to ring the church bells in his parish church. Here was a 'good work', Bunyan reasoned, which might help him gain favour with God. But it didn't bring him peace. Instead, he became afraid that the tall stone tower that housed the big, heavy bells would suddenly collapse and fall on top of him. Not only would he be crushed, he would be lost forever. The collapse of the tower was never that likely; in fact, it is still standing today! We might smile. But Bunyan knew that sin was serious, that it led to judgment, and that there was nothing he could do to save himself. For him, and indeed for us, these things are no laughing matter.

Thank God for Jesus! For although we can't do anything to save ourselves, he has done everything to make our salvation possible. Our reading from Galatians emphasises this. No one can be justified – made right with God – by their own efforts. Yet the good news is that Jesus has died for us. He was even cursed on the 'tree' (v13, NLT), the cross, that we might be forgiven. How do we receive this salvation? By doing something difficult? By trying to make ourselves acceptable to God? Absolutely not. Rather we put our faith in Jesus, and receive the Holy Spirit as a gift.

Don't take the counsel of modern 'Worldly-wisemen'. Nothing we can do will save us and make us true Christians. We rely entirely on Christ's amazing grace.

TO PONDER ...

'Amazing grace, how sweet the sound,
that saved a wretch like me.
I once was lost, but now am found.
Was blind, but now I see'

Look up the famous hymn *Amazing Grace* by John Newton and reflect on the words. We are saved by grace from first to last. If we appreciate this, it is a sure way to guard against pride. Whatever progress we make in the Christian life, however much we grow in holiness and use our gifts in God's service, it's all because of His grace.

PRAYER

Lord, I praise You for Your amazing grace. Thank You that Your Son, Jesus, did everything to make my salvation possible. Help me to appreciate this more deeply, and depend on Your continuing grace day by day. Amen.

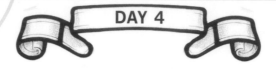

DAY 4

An open door

Matthew 7:8; John 6:37

When Evangelist realises what has happened, he challenges Christian. Why did he follow Worldly-wiseman? But when he sees Christian's genuine sorrow and despair, he explains that 'all manner of sin and blasphemies shall be forgiven unto men' and encourages Christian not to be 'faithless, but believing'. He emphasises it is only through God's grace in Jesus that he can be rid of his burden and receive eternal life.

Christian is truly sorry for his error and begs forgiveness. He then asks Evangelist if there is still hope for him. Can he 'go back, and go up to the wicket gate'? Evangelist replies that while his sin 'is very great', the man at the gate will receive him for he is full of 'good-will' towards others. After warning him to stay on the right path, Evangelist speaks words of encouragement and sends him on his way. Christian, keen not to make another mistake, heads resolutely towards the wicket gate.

So, in process of time, Christian got up to the gate. Now, over the gate there was written,

'Knock, and it shall be opened unto you.'

He knocked, therefore, more than once or twice, saying,

May I now enter here? Will he within
Open to sorry me, though I have been
An undeserving rebel? Then shall I
Not fail to sing his lasting praise on high.

At last there came a grave person to the gate, named Good-will, who asked, who was there? and whence he came? and what he would have?

CHRISTIAN: Here is a poor burdened sinner. I come from the City of Destruction, but am going to Mount Zion, that I may be delivered from the wrath to come. I would therefore, Sir, since I am informed that by this gate is the way thither, know if you are willing to let me in!

GOOD-WILL: I am willing with all my heart, said he; and with that he opened the gate.

There are many reasons why Christian *shouldn't* be allowed through the wicket gate. As he himself puts it, he is an 'undeserving rebel' and a 'poor, burdened sinner'. But Jesus has died and risen again! So, not only is the gate opened, but Christian is pulled through. Imagine how he must have felt at this moment – his anxiety turning to joy. Christ doesn't just allow him through, He *wants* him to come through.

It's not just this one pilgrim who can come, the way is open for all. Bunyan spent much of his ministry insisting that God receives all who come to Him in true repentance and faith. The title of one of his books, *Come and Welcome to Christ Jesus*, sums up this vital theme of his ministry. Do you remember Christian's wife and children who were left behind in the City of Destruction? Christiana tried to discourage and stop her husband, but one day she would lead her children through the wicket gate too. Bunyan writes beautifully and powerfully about the journey of Christiana and her family in the *The Pilgrim's Progress Part II*. Our Bible verses today show us that Bunyan knew God's heart for every one of us. Jesus will 'never drive away' anyone who comes to him (John 6:37). Those who 'seek' will 'find' and, as the words over the wicket gate say, for those who knock, 'the door will be opened' (Matthew 7:8).

If you're reading this and you're still not certain that God loves you, wants to forgive you and save you, then today's readings – both from Bunyan and the Bible – speak powerfully. You may have made a real mess of things. Perhaps, like Christian, you heard the Bible message of grace and forgiveness, but then wandered away to a very different path, rejecting God altogether. Because of Jesus' death, the way is still open for you. Jesus is ready to welcome you back!

TO PONDER …

Christian talks about singing God's praises, and this will be a recurring theme on our journey through *The Pilgrim's Progress*. Remembering all God has done and all He continues to do for us is a great stimulus to worship. He has saved us. So take time to praise Him and thank Him now.

PRAYER

Lord, thank You for the welcome You have given to me. Thank You as well that You receive all who come to You in faith because of Your great grace in Jesus. I worship You, Lord and Saviour. Amen.

Grace

Philippians 1:3–6; 2 Corinthians 12:9–10

Christian's entry in at the wicket gate is his actual point of conversion, although it is not where he loses his burden. This, Good-will tells him, he must 'be content to bear' until he comes to 'the place of deliverance' (the cross) where it will fall from his back itself. This may not be what we expect, for it is common to think of conversion and deliverance as all one. But for Christian – as it was for Bunyan himself – this is not to be. Before he arrives at the cross, Christian must visit the house of the Interpreter where he will be instructed in matters of a spiritual nature.

The house of the Interpreter is symbolic of the work of the Holy Spirit in us. The Holy Spirit often works through our spiritual guides and mentors here on earth. For Bunyan, one such 'Interpreter' was his pastor John Gifford.

In the following scene Christian is shown how Christ, through His Spirit, maintains the work of grace in the soul.

Then I saw in my dream that the Interpreter took Christian by the hand, and led him into a place where [there] was a fire burning against a wall, and one standing by it, always casting much water upon it, to quench it; yet did the fire burn higher and hotter.

Then said Christian, What means this?

The Interpreter answered, This fire is the work of grace that is wrought in the heart; he that casts water upon it, to extinguish and put it out, is the Devil; but as thou seest the fire burns higher and hotter, thou shalt also see the reason for that. So he took him about to the backside of the wall, where he saw a man with a vessel of oil in his hand, which he did also continually cast, but secretly, into the fire.

Then said Christian, What means this?

The Interpreter answered, This is Christ, who continually, with the oil of his grace, maintains the work already begun in the heart: by the means of which, notwithstanding what the devil can do, the souls of his people prove gracious still. And as thou sawest that the man stood behind the wall to maintain the fire, that is to teach thee that it is hard for the tempted to see how this work of grace is maintained in the soul.

Christian has faced some challenges already on his path to the wicket gate, and he will face many more as he presses on towards the Celestial City. His journey is hazardous, dangerous even. Bunyan describes it as a 'desperate journey'. How will Christian survive, let alone thrive? How will he negotiate the hazards and unhelpful companions? And what about the temptation simply to give up and turn back?

The answer to these questions is found in today's wonderfully encouraging extract from *The Pilgrim's Progress*. God is at work! The devil pours cold water on the faith of Christian believers, but Jesus is 'continually' at work pouring oil on the fire to keep it burning brightly. God's grace to us is truly astounding. He turns our lives around, forgives us and gives us a new start. But His grace doesn't stop there. He continues to work in us. He keeps on forgiving and He begins to transform us. He starts with us, 'just as we are' but He doesn't leave us here: He gives us the power to change, step by step. He protects us and keeps us. Paul sums it up: God who 'began a good work' in us 'will carry it on to completion'. God's grace to us in the past was wonderful, but we don't need to look back longingly. There is amazing grace for us today and tomorrow too.

One of the ways God shows His grace is to strengthen us when we are weak. This was really important to Bunyan, who often felt weak himself and wanted to encourage other Christians who might be struggling. The words of 2 Corinthians 12:9, 'My grace is sufficient for you, for my power is made perfect in weakness' are some of the most important in *The Pilgrim's Progress*. Even the apostle Paul, who wrote those words, felt weak, but God's grace was sufficient, giving him power and strength. Jesus was at work pouring oil on to Paul's faith. With Jesus stoking and fanning the flames, they would never go out. The promise is the same for us: 'he who began a good work in you will carry it on to completion' (Philippians 1:6).

TO PONDER ...

Think of the areas of your life where you feel weak, and where you feel tempted. Then think of Jesus pouring oil on to the fire of your faith, making the flames burn brighter. His grace and His power is at work. Pray for Him to strengthen you today, and pray with confidence, for God has promised to be at work in your life.

PRAYER

Lord, I praise You that Your grace is sufficient for me! Thank You, not only for saving me but also for protecting me day by day, and helping me to grow as a Christian. Help me in the areas where I feel especially weak. Strengthen me with Your mighty power, I pray. Amen.

DAY 6

The power of the cross

John 3:16; 1 Peter 2:22–24

Christian completes his time at 'the house of the Interpreter' and goes on his way, grateful for the lessons he has learnt. Having been instructed in important spiritual truths, he is now ready to come to 'the place of Deliverance'. This is a crucial scene in *The Pilgrim's Progress* and wonderfully memorable.

> *Now I saw in my dream, that the high way up which Christian was to go, was fenced on either side with a wall, and that wall was called Salvation. Up this way, therefore, did burdened Christian run, but not without great difficulty, because of the load on his back.*
>
> *He ran thus till he came at a place somewhat ascending, and upon that place stood a cross, and a little below, in the bottom, a sepulchre [tomb]. So I saw in my dream, that just as Christian came up to the cross, his burden loosed from off his shoulders, and fell from off his back, and began to tumble, and so continued to do, till it came to the mouth of the sepulchre, where it fell in, and I saw it no more.*

There is tremendous power in the cross of Christ. Bunyan brings this out brilliantly in a pivotal scene in the unfolding story of *The Pilgrim's Progress*. Use your imagination to help you identify with Christian as he experiences the joy of salvation. He climbs wearily up the steep path, painful step by painful step, the crushing burden of sin still on his back. At last he reaches the place where there is a cross and a sepulchre (the empty tomb). Jesus has died and is risen! Hallelujah! And then, suddenly, the crippling burden is 'loosed' from off his shoulders. Christian does not take it off himself; at the cross it just falls away. Imagine how he would feel, the immense relief and joy of being released from this awful heavy weight. It tumbles down the hill and disappears into the mouth of the tomb, never to be seen again.

Have the sins of Christian believers really been dealt with in this way? Is the gospel really as amazing as this? The answer is yes! The Bible tells us that because of Jesus' sacrificial death for us, we have forgiveness of sins. In fact, both sin and guilt have been dealt with through the death of Jesus, through the shedding of His blood. The cross is powerful indeed.

How do we respond to this? First, it is important to pause and consider the high price Jesus paid to win our salvation, removing our burden of sin forever. The cross of which the Bible and Bunyan speak was a terrible way to die. Two thousand years of tradition have blurred our understanding of what it was really like. We think of the cross as a beautiful ornament for the home or as something to hang around our necks. But no one in Jesus' day regarded it in these ways. Rather, it was a drawn out, shameful and immensely painful way to die. But Jesus did not only suffer humiliation and physical agony. As we read in 1 Peter, He also 'bore our sins in his body' when He died. In doing so he endured the punishment for sin that was rightfully ours. As we develop our understanding of grace, we can helpfully think of it as 'God's Riches At Christ's Expense'. At the cross we see how great the 'expense' was. There can be no higher cost.

But secondly – and gloriously – we see God's riches have been lavished on us! Sin really has been dealt with. Yes, we continue to get things wrong every day and so we need to come to God regularly in confession. But if we have truly trusted in Jesus as Saviour and Lord, there is no doubt that forgiveness is ours. The burden has gone! Sometimes we struggle because things we have done in the past still weigh heavily upon us. We have asked for forgiveness many times but we find it difficult to believe that God has really made us clean. But He has. We 'have' salvation and forgiveness, as both Bunyan and the Bible remind us. That is the wonder of God's grace. That is the power of the cross.

TO PONDER ...

Think of your sins as a terrible heavy burden on your back. You try to pull the burden from off your back but however hard you struggle, it's impossible. There's simply nothing you can do. Then imagine that the cords, which hold the burden so firmly in place, snap. The heavy weight has gone. Someone else has set you free! How can this be? You look at the cross and the empty tomb. You watch the burden roll away and disappear through the entrance to the tomb. It is now out of sight – forever. Thank God for what He has done for you through the death and resurrection of Jesus. Know and accept in your heart that God has completely forgiven you.

PRAYER

Father, I praise You that Your Son, the Lord Jesus, died for me to win my salvation. Thank You that He was willing to pay such a high price to set me free, and that He rose again. I worship You for Your glorious grace, lavished on me. Thank You especially for Your wonderful forgiveness. My sin and guilt have been dealt with on the cross. I worship You. Amen.

Freedom in Christ

Romans 5:6–8; John 8:32

This next passage follows straight on from the previous one. Christian has lost his burden; a burden the narrator tells us will be seen 'no more'. It has gone forever, dealt with finally and completely by Christ's death on the cross. Here we experience Christian's emotional response to the realisation of Christ's 'amazing grace'.

Then was Christian glad and lightsome, and said with a merry heart, 'He hath given me rest by his sorrow, and life by his death.' Then he stood still a while, to look and wonder; for it was very surprising to him, that the sight of the cross should thus ease him of his burden. He looked, therefore, and looked again, even till the springs that were in his head sent the waters down his cheeks. Now, as he stood looking and weeping, behold three Shining Ones came to him and saluted him with, 'Peace be to thee'. So the first said to him, 'Thy sins be forgiven thee', the second stripped him of his rags, and clothed him with 'change of raiment', the third also set a mark in his forehead, and gave him a roll with a seal upon it, which he bade him look on as he ran, and that he should give it in at the Celestial Gate. So they went their way. Then Christian gave three leaps for joy, and went on singing

As Christian stands looking at the cross, with the great weight of his burden removed, he is overcome. In one of Bunyan's most beautiful lines we read that the 'springs that were in his head sent the waters down his cheeks'. Christian wept tears of immense relief, which gave way to joy. The pent up emotion just came flooding out. Then angels come to him and reassure him of God's peace and forgiveness.

He is given clean clothes to wear. He has assurance he now belongs to God. Before, he had to struggle to take each step, his back almost broken by his wearisome burden. Now he can run! No wonder that he gave three leaps for joy and went on his way singing.

Joy is one of the key notes of the Christian life, or at least that's what the Bible tells us. Sometimes Christians can be thoroughly miserable people, yet the Bible is packed full of joyful emotion. Its key characters, such as Peter and Paul, knew much suffering yet their lives were characterised by much rejoicing too, and they urge other Christians to rejoice as well (as we see in 1 Peter 1:6; Philippians 4:4). The psalms cover every human feeling, but exuberant praise is often to the fore (as we see in Psalm 150). What about us? Are our lives characterised by the joy of which the Bible speaks, and that Bunyan's pilgrim feels so deeply?

How do we get this joy? Some people try and work themselves into a joyful state, focusing on their feelings. But this is not the way forward. Notice what happens to Christian in today's passage. It is when he fixes his eyes on the cross that the tears well up and begin to flow. So it is with us. When we look to the cross and reflect on all it means for us, the joy starts to flow. Peace, forgiveness and assurance: these things and more are ours because of the cross of Christ.

If you're not feeling joyful as you read this don't feel crushed or condemned. We all go through times when we feel low, sometimes because of circumstances, sometimes because we have a tendency to feel down. But the encouragement here is to contemplate all that God has done for you in Jesus. When we do this, so often happiness does come. Whatever we go through in this life, we are clean, forgiven and secure in our relationship with Jesus. We are on our way to heaven – the 'Celestial City'. Such knowledge transforms the way we live in the present, not least by making us people with a deep happiness. When was the last time you took three leaps for joy? If you contemplate the cross and what it means for you for long enough, you might find it hard to limit yourself to three!

TO PONDER ...

Has your life lost some of its sparkle and joy? Take some time, either today or on some future occasion, to reflect on today's Bible verses from Romans 5, and our passage from *The Pilgrim's Progress*. God has done this for you! Whatever life throws at you, no one can take these things away. Start praising God for what He has done. Who knows, the feelings of joy might start flowing quicker than you think.

PRAYER

Lord, thank You for all You've done for me in Jesus. As I contemplate You and all You have given me, flood my life with Your joy. Amen.

Better though difficult the right way to go

Challenges ahead

CHRISTIAN · CLIMBS · THE · HILL · DIFFICULTY

Springs of water

Isaiah 49:10–11; John 4:10–15

Christian eagerly continues on his way, soon sighting three sleeping men called Simple, Sloth and Presumption. As always with Bunyan, the characters live up to their names. Offers of help and counselling in the ways of God fall on deaf ears and the men go back to sleep. Christian then meets two more men, Formalist and Hypocrisy, who have tumbled over a wall to join the pathway to heaven. They have not come in by the gate and so, Christian warns them, they 'are counted thieves already, by the Lord of the way' and they will not be saved. Concerned for their spiritual welfare, he tells them about his experience at the cross but they simply laugh at him and walk on by. So Christian goes on alone, taking regular encouragement as he reads the roll given to him at the cross.

I beheld, then, that they all went on till they came to the foot of the Hill Difficulty; at the bottom of which was a spring. There was also in the same place two other ways besides that which came straight from the gate; one turned to the left hand, and the other to the right, at the bottom of the hill; but the narrow way lay right up the hill, and the name of the going up the side of the hill, is called Difficulty. Christian now went to the spring, and drank thereof, to refresh himself, and then began to go up the hill, saying:

The hill, though high, I covet to ascend,
The difficulty will not me offend;
For I perceive the way to life lies here.
Come, pluck up heart, let's neither faint nor fear;

Better, though difficult, the right way to go,
Than wrong, though easy, where the end is woe.

Yesterday we read of the springs of water that Christian wept as he stood at the cross, freed at last from his great burden. These tears were no doubt shed with a mix of emotions: grief for his past life and sadness at not being able to share this moment with his loved ones, relief that his burden is gone forever, and joy that his sins are forgiven. Christian knows with utter certainty now that he has a new and eternal hope in Christ. His tears release emotions that enable him to continue his journey with a freedom and a joy that has so far eluded him. His tears are healing tears. He is indeed a new man.

Today we read of a different 'spring', a spring of water for pilgrims to drink from before they tackle the steep ascent of the 'hill' called 'Difficulty'. Its purpose seems obvious and very sensible. Climbing mountains requires more physical strength than walking on flat ground and therefore more sustenance, especially water. But this spring is different. It is more than a supply of water for physical energy; it is a spring for spiritual renewal and refreshment. Christian has a spiritual mountain to climb and he needs Christ, the 'living water' to help him. As Christian drinks from it, he grows in both courage and conviction. He knows this will be difficult, but he knows it is the right path. And now he also knows he will have the help he needs through Christ to get him to the top. So the pilgrim is able to approach this challenging ascent with conviction and eagerness.

So it is with us. We know, as Christians, that we will suffer, for Jesus calls us to take up our cross daily and follow Him (Luke 9:23). We know that we will have our own 'Hill Difficulty' – in fact we will likely have many more than one. But we also know we have God on our side, a God who is sovereign, a God who knows us better than we know ourselves. He will not send us any trial we are unable to bear. God loves each and every one of us so much that He sent his only Son, Jesus Christ, to die on the cross that we might have eternal life. Like Bunyan's pilgrim, we too can drink from the spring. This is Christ, the 'living water', and He will freely give.

TO PONDER ...

God has supplied us with both physical and spiritual water. He has given us water to drink to keep us healthy in body, mind and spirit. Now consider for a moment. Do you drink enough water? Do you let yourself cry 'healing tears' when you need to? Do you drink enough of Christ, your 'living water'? God has given you 'springs of water' for your good. Are you making the most of them?

PRAYER

Father, thank You for giving me springs of water. Thank You for the wonder of creation, for Your wisdom in and love for all creation. You know my every need and You supply it. Open my eyes that I may see more clearly the daily expressions of Your love and care. Whether You are leading me by still waters or up hills of 'Difficulty', strengthen me by Your Spirit and help me to drink afresh each day from Your springs of living water. Amen.

Keeping hold of assurance

1 John 4:13–16; Ephesians 1:13,14

Christian, as we have seen, takes refreshment from the spring and begins the steep ascent of the hill. Formalist and Hypocrisy spy two other, seemingly easier, ways up the hill. But these ways are not easier. Like their names, they are full of Danger and Destruction and the two pilgrims stumble and die.

The Hill Difficulty is just that – difficult! But God lovingly supplies true pilgrims with help and refreshment along the way, so it is not long before Christian comes to 'a pleasant arbour', a resting place. Here Christian sits down to rest and to read the roll that was given him by the Shining Ones at the cross. But instead he falls into a deep sleep and drops it. He wakes with a start and rushes on his way, concerned that he has lost valuable time. Only when he reaches the top of the hill does he realise he has lost his precious roll. Christian is horrified and in great distress he retraces his steps, desperate to find his roll, his pass to the Celestial City.

> *Now by this time he was come to the arbour again, where for a while he sat down and wept; but at last, as Christian would have it, looking sorrowfully down under the settle, there he espied his roll; the which he, with trembling and haste, catched up, and put it into his bosom. But who can tell how joyful this man was when he had gotten his roll again! For this roll was the assurance of his life and acceptance at the desired haven. Therefore he laid it up in his bosom, gave thanks to God for directing his eye to the place where it lay, and with joy and tears betook himself again to his journey.*

Do we have assurance of salvation? Do we know that we really belong to God, and are saved by Him? For a period of time, Christian doubted this and was thoroughly unhappy. This mirrors John Bunyan's own experience. For a number of years, he doubted that God loved him. Yes, the gospel was true, but was it really for him? He believed there was no hope for him and, unsurprisingly, was plunged into a pit of despair.

We can doubt God's love as well, perhaps particularly after a series of discouragements that have set us back. Christian went through a really difficult period before he lost his roll, that is, his assurance of salvation. The characters he meets, like Hypocrisy, are of no help to him. He finds himself alone. Perhaps it's no surprise that he begins to doubt God's love. Maybe you have begun to doubt because of similar circumstances. Or perhaps the reasons that have caused your lack of certainty are different. Whatever the reason, we can all struggle with truly believing that God loves us, and that Jesus died for us all personally.

If we've trusted Jesus for our salvation, we belong to Him and not even losing our sense of assurance can change this. But it's really helpful to keep hold of assurance, because if we're anxious about this truth, it's hard to grow in our relationship with Jesus. And the joy that is the hallmark of the Christian life will most likely be missing. Perhaps we could think of 1 John 4:13–16 as our 'roll'. The apostle John says we can 'know' we are secure in God's love. The focus in these verses is primarily on what God has done. He has sent Jesus to be the Saviour of the world. He has poured the Holy Spirit into our lives. God has promised this to all who have trusted Him, therefore it *has* happened. Look again at the Bible readings for today and be assured of His presence. Most of all, He loves us, and we can rely on that love, for it is there for us at all times. Do we trust Him? He invites us to believe in the promises of His Word, the Bible, and take up our roll once again. When we do this, our tears of despair can turn to tears of joy.

TO PONDER …

It's near impossible to grow in a relationship when we don't trust the other person. God says He loves us and invites us to put our faith in His promise. Think of 1 John 4:13–16 as your 'roll', your assurance, today. You may want to write down these verses and keep them with you. Put your trust in God once again as you turn to Him in prayer.

PRAYER

Lord, thank You that You love me, and thank You that You sent Your Son, the Lord Jesus, to be my Saviour. I praise You that You gave me the faith to believe and I thank You that I can trust and rely on You. Help me to keep believing even in times of great discouragement. Give me joy and peace in my growing relationship with You, I pray. Amen.

Peace

John 14:25–27; Philippians 4:4–7

Christian, once again in possession of his roll, is able to climb easily up the rest of the hill. But as the sun goes down, he is reminded of his mistake in falling asleep and sees the approaching darkness as punishment. But he is mistaken. Looking up, he beholds 'a very stately palace before him, the name of which was Beautiful'. He walks towards it, eager to see if he can lodge there for the night but, spying the two lions guarding the palace, he becomes afraid. The porter of the palace, Watchful, reassures him that the lions are chained and placed there to guard against false pilgrims, so Christian is able to walk safely through. Watchful explains that the palace was built by God 'for the relief and security of pilgrims'. He then introduces Christian to a woman called Discretion. Assured that Christian is 'blessed of the Lord', Discretion invites him in to meet her sisters and the rest of the family.

So when he was come in and sat down, they gave him something to drink, and consented together, that until supper was ready, some of them should have some particular discourse with Christian, for the best improvement of time; and they appointed Piety, and Prudence, and Charity to discourse with him; and thus they began ...

Thus they discoursed together till late at night; and after they had committed themselves to their Lord for protection, they betook themselves to rest: the Pilgrim they laid in a large upper chamber, whose window opened towards the sun-rising; the name of the chamber was Peace; where he slept till break of day, and then he awoke and sang,

Where am I now? Is this the love and care
Of Jesus, for the men that Pilgrims are?
Thus to provide! that I should be forgiven!
And dwell already the next door to heaven!

Christian is only a short way into his journey, yet he has experienced many challenges: conviction of sin and the sense of despair that accompanied this, the trauma of leaving his wife and children behind, the Slough of Despond, and Worldly-wiseman. Then there was the falling asleep and losing his roll on Hill Difficulty. It really is proving to be quite a 'dangerous journey'.

But now Christian has found some 'peace' at last. He has arrived at the palace Beautiful and is given a hero's welcome. It must have felt much like a five-star hotel does at the end of a gruelling trek – a luxurious house, great food, a warm welcome – and a beautiful bedroom named 'Peace'. Just what he needs! Christian's journey may have been a dangerous one, but despite the difficulties, it has also been full of God-given 'helps': Evangelist, Help, Goodwill, springs of water, the arbour ... And now, once again, God delivers – but this time, it is in abundance. At palace Beautiful, Christian enjoys a wonderful time of rest and relaxation in the company of fellow pilgrims. He knows he is safe (the lions are outside guarding the palace), there is a plentiful supply of good food, there is much spiritual conversation (something he craves), and he is staying in a wonderfully peaceful bedroom with great views. It is not difficult to imagine how Christian must be feeling!

Let us reflect for a moment on this palace and all the qualities that it represents: beauty, peace, safety, rest, physical and spiritual refreshment, encouragement, love, friendship, truth. Finding all those qualities wrapped up in one place would be quite a challenge for us today. We might be more likely to find them shared out amongst a number of different places. But there is one place where they can all be found, a place that doesn't require us to travel far or pay out lots of money to get to. We have our own 'palace Beautiful' on our doorstep: it is Christ our Saviour. He is beauty, peace, rest and refreshment. He is encouragement, love and friendship. He is 'the way and the truth and the life' (John 14:6). And He is here with us now, by the Spirit. To have life in abundance, Christ just requires us to come to Him, to 'knock' at His door and drink the 'living water'.

TO PONDER ...

The Bible teaches that Christ is 'the head of the body, the church' (Colossians 1:18). When Bunyan described the palace Beautiful, he was actually thinking of his own church in Bedford and churches like it. In a time of great religious upheaval, such churches were (for Bunyan and many others) places of spiritual rest and refreshment in the comfort and company of fellow pilgrims; places where belie vers could feel spiritually at 'peace'.

Take a moment to reflect. Consider your church in the light of each of the qualities ascribed to palace Beautiful. Then, consider your personal contribution to your church. Is there anything you can do to enhance just one of these qualities?

PRAYER

Take a moment to pray for your church and pray about your own contribution to it.

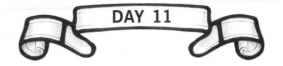

Our sword and our shield

Romans 8:35–39; Ephesians 6:10–17

Christian enjoys a wonderful time of rest and relaxation at the palace Beautiful, enjoying the company of fellow believers. Whilst there, he is able to spend time in spiritual conversation that both encourages and challenges him. He talks of his home in the City of Destruction, his experience at the cross and his pain at leaving his wife and children. He is also taken into the armoury and supplied with such spiritual armour, 'as sword, shield, helmet, breastplate, all-prayer, and shoes that would not wear out'.

Christian is soon to realise the importance of this armour. On leaving the palace, he almost immediately finds himself in the Valley of Humiliation where he comes face to face with the devil Apollyon. A fierce spiritual battle ensues. Christian resists 'as manfully as he could' but Apollyon proves a terrible enemy. And so Christian, 'by reason of his wounds', becomes weaker and weaker.

Then Apollyon, espying his opportunity, began to gather up close to Christian, and wrestling with him, gave him a dreadful fall; and with that, Christian's sword flew out of his hand. Then said Apollyon, I am sure of thee now. And with that he had almost pressed him to death; so that Christian began to despair of life: but as God would have it, while Apollyon was fetching of his last blow, thereby to make a full end of this good man, Christian nimbly reached out his hand for his sword, and caught it, saying, 'Rejoice not against me, O mine enemy: when I fall, I shall arise'; and with that gave him a deadly thrust, which made him give back, as one that had received his mortal wound. Christian perceiving that, made at him again, saying,

'Nay, in all these things we are more than conquerors, through Him that loved us'. And with that Apollyon spread forth his dragon's wings, and sped him away, that Christian for a season saw him no more.

We now realise there was an additional purpose to Christian's time of refreshment and renewal at the palace Beautiful. We already know it was a time of safety and comfort after many dangerous experiences on the first part of his journey, and that it provided him with much needed rest immediately after climbing Hill Difficulty. But it was also vital preparation for his terrible encounter with the fiend Apollyon.

There is a lesson here for all of us, just as there was for Christian. Periods of calm and ease can soon be shaken by new challenges, difficult circumstances, immense suffering. The Bible tells us that the Christian journey will not be easy. It is a 'narrow' path with many rough places along the way, so we must be prepared. At the palace Beautiful Christian is not only given time to re-energise; he is also given armour. This is spiritual armour for a spiritual battle. He didn't realise at the time just how necessary this armour would be, nor how soon he would need it. This is why the Bible tells us to 'put on the full armour of God' (Ephesians 6:13). We don't know when, or where, or how we will need it; all we know is that we will need it, so we need to be ready.

The thought of a spiritual battle such as the one described here is pretty terrifying. But just as we should be prepared, we should not be alarmed. Why? Because God is greater. The devil may win the battle, but God will win the war! God is in control even when it feels like He isn't. Whatever battles we face, whatever trials we go through, God knows, God cares *and* God prevails. God is our greatest weapon against the wiles of the devil, for 'If God is for us, who can be against us?' (Romans 8:31).

In the final moments of his battle with Apollyon, we are told that Christian calls upon two pieces of armour in particular: the shield of faith, which protects him from Apollyon's flaming darts; and the sword of the Spirit, which enables Christian to get rid of Apollyon.

We must do the same. In all circumstances we should have our sword (the Word of God) and our shield ready. We must be prepared; but we should not be alarmed. 'No, in all these things we are more than conquerors through him who loved us' (Romans 8:37).

TO PONDER ...

The thought of a spiritual battle can be frightening. Are there spiritual battles that you are facing in your own life right now? Remember that God gives you armour; spiritual armour for a spiritual battle. He gives us the means of protection, but in order for it to be effective we need to have it ready in all circumstances.

PRAYER

Father, thank You that You equip me for spiritual warfare. Help me to use the spiritual 'weapons' You give me. And thank You that, by the Spirit, You stand with me and fight for me. I praise You that with You, I am on the victorious side. Amen.

All-prayer

Psalm 23:4; Ephesians 6:18

Christian had fought Apollyon and won. He gives thanks to God for delivering him and is immediately supplied with leaves from the tree of life to heal his wounds. After taking some refreshment, he continues on his way. This time he has his sword drawn and at the ready – his encounter with Apollyon has taught him that he must always be prepared.

At the end of the Valley of Humiliation is another valley, the Valley of the Shadow of Death. The path to the Celestial City lies through the middle of this valley, so there is no avoiding it. It is a terrible and dangerous place where many pilgrims, we are told, have 'miserably perished'. The challenge that Christian faces now is worse than his fight with Apollyon.

The pathway was here also exceeding narrow, and therefore good Christian was the more put to it; for when he sought, in the dark, to shun the ditch on the one hand, he was ready to tip over into the mire on the other; also when he sought to escape the mire, without great carefulness he would be ready to fall into the ditch. Thus he went on, and I heard him here sigh bitterly; for besides the dangers mentioned above, the pathway was here so dark, that ofttimes, when he lift up his foot to set forward, he knew not where, or upon what he should set it next.

About the midst of this valley, I perceived the mouth of hell to be, and it stood also hard by the way-side. Now, thought Christian, what shall I do? And ever and anon the flame and smoke would come out in such abundance, with sparks and hideous noises (things that cared not for Christian's sword, as did Apollyon before), that he was forced to put up his sword, and betake himself to another weapon, called All-prayer. So he cried in my hearing, 'O Lord, I beseech thee, deliver my soul!'

Christian is surrounded by difficulties on all sides. With powerful language Bunyan builds his picture of the struggle the alarmed pilgrim is facing: the mire on one side, the ditch on the other, the narrow dark pathway, the flames and the smoke ...

This happens to us. Of course, there can be times in our lives when our Christian 'pilgrimage' is much easier. The path is smooth, the way ahead is clear, our friends are with us. Yet, for most of us, there are times when the path is rough and steep, we feel very much alone and the darkness has descended. We're not sure where to put our foot next. We just can't see the way.

The solution, says Bunyan, is prayer. Some today may laugh at this. But the Bible, once again, agrees with Bunyan. When the going gets tough, the tough get praying! To pray in difficult times is also to engage in real spiritual warfare. We hammer on the gates of heaven and ask God to help us and others who are in difficulty. We wrestle with God in prayer. This is the only way we can stay on the path.

If you are facing difficulties today, turn to prayer now. He is your help and deliverance. And pray for others too: 'always keep on praying for all the Lord's people' (Ephesians 6:18). Giving ourselves to intercession is a sign of mature Christian faith. It is the strong Christian who knows that 'All-prayer' is their greatest weapon. In the battles that we face, we need to keep this weapon close by our side. Much more than that, we need to use it daily.

TO PONDER ...

'What a Friend we have in Jesus, all our sins and griefs to bear!
What a privilege to carry everything to God in prayer!
O what peace we often forfeit, O what needless pain we bear,
All because we do not carry everything to God in prayer.

Have we trials and temptations? Is there trouble anywhere?
We should never be discouraged; take it to the Lord in prayer.
Can we find a friend so faithful who will all our sorrows share?
Jesus knows our every weakness; take it to the Lord in prayer.'
(Joseph M. Scriven, 1819–1896)

PRAYER

Lord, thank You that I can bring everything to You in prayer. Help me to engage in spiritual warfare daily, not only praying for myself but also for others. Today I pray that You would help me in the struggles I face, and also that You would help my friends who are finding the way ahead right now dark and difficult. Strengthen them and bring them through. Amen.

Deliverance

Psalm 23; 39:12; 139:7–12

Christian confronts many dreadful and fearful sights as he journeys through the Valley of the Shadow of Death. Remembering how he has conquered many dangers already, and thinking that going back may be even more dangerous, he resolves to go on 'in the strength of the Lord'. It is not an easy journey and Christian soon begins to feel discouraged again. But then he hears the voice of a fellow pilgrim in the distance, speaking the words of Psalm 23. There are fellow pilgrims in the Valley and soon he might have companionship. This is a great encouragement to Christian.

Then the night breaks into day, bringing further hope to the weary pilgrim. Looking back, Christian can now see more clearly the dangers he has come through. He thanks God for deliverance. Although he can see there are even greater dangers ahead, he knows that 'by his light I go through darkness' and can journey on with confidence. He begins to sing …

O world of wonders! (I can say no less)
That I should be preserv'd in that distress
That I have met with here! O blessed be
That hand that from it hath deliver'd me!
Dangers in darkness, devils, hell, and sin,
Did compass me, while I this Vale was in:
Yea, snares and pits, and traps, and nets, did lie
My path about, that worthless, silly I
Might have been catch'd, entangled, and cast down;
But since I live, let JESUS wear the crown.

Christian has travelled through a valley full of terrible 'Snares, and Pits, and Traps, and Nets'. He describes himself, rather quaintly to our ears, as a 'worthless silly' (of course he isn't, for God loves him and has called him). Perhaps we too can relate to Christian's negative self-assessment – we often feel bad about ourselves when we struggle through difficulties along our own journey of faith. But Christian can now see that not only has God protected him through this dark and terrible valley, He has delivered him too. Night has turned to day. No wonder he bursts into joyful song.

God protects and delivers us too. Psalm 23 has been proved true time and again in the experience of Christians. God is with us in the darkest valley and he brings us through. We experience darkness, but then the light begins to shine. Of course, if we're in the middle of a dark valley right now, it can be hard to appreciate this. But God is with us even if it does not seem like it, for 'even the darkness will not be dark to [God]' (Psalm 139:12). And He *does* lead us through. Darkness, suffering, death … none of this has the last word for those who love Jesus. That last word always belongs to Him, who is the 'light of the world' and the 'resurrection and the life' (John 8:12; 11:25).

Think about a time when God has been with you in the past, and has brought you through a terrible trial. Think about how He delivered you, and give thanks to Him. Notice how Christian gives all the glory to God for his deliverance. He lives, so he wants Jesus to wear the crown; he wants God to have the glory. As we give thanks to God for His protection and His help, our faith is strengthened and we trust Him more for the future. Christian knew there were dangers ahead and that there would be many more obstacles to overcome on his pilgrimage, but still he sings. That is a sign of great faith. Bunyan's pilgrim has known God's deliverance and so, joyfully, he believes God will do it again. This joyful trust in God is an example to us. In the valley, his faith has been strengthened.

TO PONDER ...

'When through fiery trials your pathway shall lie,
My grace all-sufficient shall be your supply;
The flame shall not hurt you: I only design
Your dross to consume, and your gold to refine.'
('K' in John Rippon's *A Selection of Hymns*, 1787)

PRAYER

Thank You, Lord, for all the times You have protected me and brought me through difficulties. I know that You are a faithful God. I put my faith in You and the promises of Your Word once again. I trust You to bring me through today, whatever I face. And I trust You for the future, too. Amen.

Is thy strength so small? Fear not the lions

Transformed lives

CHRISTIAN · APPROACHES · THE · HOUSE · BEAUTIFUL

An active faith

Psalm 119:33–40; James 1:22

Christian has come safely through the Valley of the Shadow of Death. He soon meets Faithful, a former neighbour from the City of Destruction, who has set off on his own pilgrimage of faith. They greet each other warmly, both very happy to have the company of a fellow traveller, and continue on together, sharing stories and experiences of their journeys so far and the different characters they have met along the way.

As they walk on, they meet up with a character called Talkative. Talkative is happy to speak about Christian things; indeed, he seems very knowledgeable about anything 'spiritual'. But when Faithful questions him about the impact of faith, Talkative is uncomfortable and his answers are brief and evasive. Faithful, on the other hand, is able to talk about the Christian life with a depth of sincerity that eludes Talkative. In today's passage from *The Pilgrim's Progress*, Faithful speaks about the importance of a living relationship with God through Jesus, and how we need to put the knowledge we have into practice.

FAITHFUL: for knowledge, great knowledge, may be obtained in the mysteries of the gospel, and yet no work of grace in the soul. Yea, if a man have all knowledge, he may yet be nothing, and so consequently be no child of God. When Christ said, 'Do you know all these things?' and the disciples had answered, Yes; he addeth, 'Blessed are ye if ye do them.' He doth not lay the blessing in the knowing of them, but in the doing of them. For there is a knowledge that is not attended with doing: 'He that knoweth his master's will, and doth it not.' A man may know like an angel, and yet be no Christian, therefore your sign of it is not true. Indeed, to KNOW, is a thing that pleaseth talkers and boasters; but TO DO is that which pleaseth God.

Here we have both a serious warning and a strong challenge. The warning is about the dangers of a particular type of knowledge. On one level, Talkative is extremely knowledgeable. He really knows about God and Christian things. Ask him a question about God and he will give you a sermon – often a very long one! What's more, some of what he says is correct. But, despite this seemingly impressive knowledge, something vital is missing. He does not have a living relationship with Jesus Christ. He knows much about God, but he does not know him personally. Such a person, as Faithful puts it, is 'no child of God'.

Of course, it's good to know *about* God and His ways, but this is no substitute for *knowing* Him personally and deeply. We talk sometimes about the difference between 'head knowledge' and 'heart knowledge'; the difference between what we understand with our minds, and the personal knowledge that fires the heart. We need both. Yes, let's study hard so we can learn as much as we can about our Lord, but let's be like Faithful rather than Talkative. Let's press on to know God deeply and intimately. This is the type of knowledge that pleases God.

There is a further step we must take. Faithful's words summon us to action. They call us not only *to know* God's will but also *to do* it. This is the strong challenge Bunyan gives us. Our knowledge of God and His Word should impact every area of our lives. No part is to be left untouched. True knowledge of God leads to personal renewal, as Psalm 119 reminds us. And, as both today's Bible readings tell us, we are to do what God commands. Real knowledge of God will work itself out in a changed life.

So the message is clear: imitate Faithful, and not Talkative! Know God personally and allow that knowledge to transform the whole of your life. Be someone who not only *knows* the Master's will, but also *does* it.

TO PONDER …

Reflect on your own knowledge of God. How well do you know Him? Resolve to press on to know Him better. And ask God for the strength, by the Holy Spirit, to be a 'doer of the Word' rather than a 'hearer' only. As you think about your life, ask God to show you areas where there might be a 'disconnect' between what you know and how you live. As God brings things to mind you might like to note them down, asking him to change you so that your life is more consistent. If you want to, use the following prayer to help you.

PRAYER

Father God, thank You that You call me into relationship with You, through Your Son Jesus. Help me to press on to know You more and more. Strengthen me by the Spirit. Make me a 'doer' of the Word and not just a 'hearer'. Amen.

A life of holiness

Colossians 3:3–4,12–14; Romans 6:1–2; Luke 10:27

Faithful and Talkative continue their conversation. Faithful has spoken of the need for an active faith, a faith spurred on by 'the grace of faith and love; which puts a man upon doing even the will of God from the heart'. Realising that Talkative has no experience of a personal relationship with Christ, Faithful is keen to help his companion understand the true meaning of a living faith. He explains that for the believer the signs of true faith will be discovered, in greater or lesser degrees, by a sense of 'joy and peace', a love of holiness, a desire to know more of God and 'to serve him in this world'. Faithful then goes on to explain what others should see in those who have confessed faith in Christ.

> *a life answerable to that confession; to wit, a life of holiness; heart-holiness, family-holiness, (if he hath a family) and by conversation-holiness in the world; which, in the general, teacheth him, inwardly, to abhor his sin, and himself for that, in secret; to suppress it in his family, and to promote holiness in the world; not by talk only, as a hypocrite or talkative person may do, but by a practical subjection, in faith and love, to the power of the Word.*

To be a Christian is to be a child of God. God has chosen us, and in return we have in a way chosen Him. He invites us; and we accept the invitation. Christian *wanted* to know what to do be 'saved'; he *wanted* to find the 'light' that Evangelist had pointed him to. It's the same with us. Like Christian in this story, we have to *want* to go on a journey with God. For some, that journey may have begun as a child and continued through without a fight; for others, the road may have been more difficult. But whatever our story, becoming a Christian is the most important event in our lives. It means our own great burden has fallen away and disappeared forever. It means we have experienced the 'amazing grace' that is offered to us through the death of Christ, and have a promise of a new and eternal hope – for this life and the next. And we have a relationship with a living, faithful, all-powerful, creator God who loves us more than we can imagine. How awesome is that? But becoming a Christian is just the start of the journey. The rest of our lives must be devoted to Jesus. To be a child of God is both an honour and a responsibility.

This is what the conversation between Faithful and Talkative is really all about. Talkative has shown himself to be fluent in the language of being a Christian, but not such an expert in the reality of it. Why not? In Bunyan's words: 'heart-work'. Talkative's faith is an intellectual one. It engages his mind and his mouth, but not his heart. To be truly Christian, the Bible tells us, is to 'Love the Lord your God with all your heart and with all your soul and with all your strength and with all your mind' (Luke 10:27). If we love God, it should follow that we will want to honour Him in every aspect of our lives. This is what Faithful is describing in today's passage. It is, in his words, a life 'answerable to that confession'. To love God is to show it. How? Through 'a life of holiness', says Faithful, 'a practical subjection, in faith and love, to the power of the Word'.

What God requires of us – and what we should require of ourselves – is exactly what Faithful describes to Talkative here: 'a life of holiness; heart-holiness, family-holiness … and conversation-holiness'. We should strive for this not because we have to but because we *want to*, even when the going gets tough or we don't like where we are going! Why? Because we love God and want to honour Him. To love God is not just to live a life of holiness; it is to love to live it!

TO PONDER ...

'The greatest need of my people is my personal holiness.' Scottish preacher, Robert Murray M'Cheyne*

PRAYER

Father, I thank You for all that You have done for me. Open the eyes of my understanding so that I might know what it means to live a life of holiness and open my heart to love You more each day so that I might love to live for You. Amen.

*www.mcheyne.info/quotes.php [Accessed June 2016]

DAY 16

True encouragement

Ezekiel 3:16–21; Matthew 28:19–20

Talkative listens to Faithful, but apparently has little to say himself. When Faithful asks Talkative if he experiences true faith and can answer in a way that 'the God above will say Amen to', Talkative blushes. He recovers from his embarrassment but refuses to be drawn into the conversation further, accusing Faithful of judging him rashly. He does not wish to spend any more time with the pilgrim and says goodbye. Talkative is symbolic of pilgrims who 'talk the talk' but do not want to 'walk the walk'. Such pilgrims, says Christian, 'do puzzle the world, blemish Christianity, and grieve the sincere' and he commends Faithful for his speaking so frankly with Talkative.

> *How Talkative at first lifts up his plumes!*
> *How bravely doth he speak! How he presumes*
> *To drive down all before him! But so soon*
> *As Faithful talks of heart-work, like the moon*
> *That's past the full, into the wane he goes.*
> *And so will all, but he that* HEART-WORK *knows.*

Faithful has indeed been upfront with Talkative, but he has done this for good reason. He has discerned that Talkative's faith is not a saving faith and is desperately concerned to help him understand this. He speaks plainly because that is what Talkative, spiritually speaking, needs most. It is also what the Bible commands us to do. Today's passage from Ezekiel is a clear reminder of our responsibility here. But Talkative is not convinced and wants nothing more to do with Faithful or Christian. He still believes his own way is as good as theirs and decides to journey on alone.

What Faithful does here is difficult and requires much discernment, wisdom and sensitivity. It can be so much easier to say nothing, change the subject or avoid such conversations altogether. However, as Christians we are not called to an easy life, nor are we called to a silent one! Occasionally, of course, silence really is the wiser option, but not always. Christ tells His disciples to 'make disciples of all nations, baptising them in the name of the Father and of the Son and of the Holy Spirit, and teaching them to obey everything that I have commanded you' (Matthew 28:19–20). This is not an instruction for the chosen few, something we can leave to ministers and missionaries. No – as Christians we are all called to be Christ's representatives here on earth. We are all called to 'make disciples'.

Was Faithful right to challenge Talkative like this? Plain speaking to another about anything sensitive can be incredibly difficult, for the speaker and for the listener. But there are times, as today's Bible reading tells us, when such plain speaking is right, appropriate and necessary. In fact, it would be wrong to do anything less. This is one such case. Talkative does not understand the true meaning of being Christian. Faithful can see this and has the opportunity to talk plainly with him – so he does. And as the conversation goes on, he becomes increasingly direct. This is not to judge Talkative or cause him offence, but to help him understand the true meaning of having faith in Christ. Faithful is simply doing what he, as a Christian believer, has been called to do. We must do the same. Whether we are called in the moment to comfort or to challenge, it is a call to which we, as believers, must have the courage to respond.

TO PONDER ...

How do you respond to today's reflection? Are there times when you have spoken when you should have been silent, or times when you have been silent when you should have spoken?

PRAYER

Father, help me to discern when I should speak and when I should be silent. In the situations where You are calling me to speak, give me the courage I need and the right words to say. Amen.

The ultimate test

FAITHFUL
HELPING CHRISTIAN

Faith that stands the test

1 Peter 1:3–9

Christian and Faithful walk on, sharing experiences along the way. They find themselves in a wilderness, a part of the journey that could have been tedious had it not been for their companionship and conversation. After some time, they see Evangelist following them. They greet each other warmly. Evangelist, as their spiritual guide, asks how they're getting on.

Then Christian and Faithful told him of all things that had happened to them in the way; and how, and with what difficulty, they had arrived to that place.

EVANGELIST: Right glad am I, said Evangelist, not that you have met with trials, but that you have been victors; and for that you have, notwithstanding many weaknesses, continued in the way to this very day.

I say, right glad am I of this thing, and that for mine own sake and yours. I have sowed, and you have reaped; and the day is coming, when both he that sowed, and they that reaped shall rejoice together; that is, if you hold out; 'for, in due season ye shall reap, if you faint not'. The crown is before you, and it is an incorruptible one; 'so run, that ye may obtain' it.

Christian and Faithful are still pressing forward on the road to the Celestial City. No wonder Evangelist rejoices when he meets them again. When we share our faith with others and they respond and really step out on the life of discipleship, it's a great joy. God gives us so many rewards as we engage in gospel work. To see people we've shared the good news with following Jesus wholeheartedly is one of the greatest rewards of all.

Evangelist is especially happy that his friends have been 'victors' through their many 'trials'. Despite their weaknesses God has helped them, and they are continuing in the life of discipleship. Their faith has remained and indeed grown as they have faced various difficulties.

It is through trials that our faith is both shown to be real and developed further. Our reading from 1 Peter 1:3–9 makes this point powerfully. We have to suffer 'grief' in all kinds of trials, but as we push through these and come out the other side, genuine faith stands the test and is strengthened. Peter uses the illustration of gold in a furnace. In the intense heat the dross is burned away and the precious metal is refined – and it is the same with us. Faith that can withstand the fire is refined, made purer. Of course, being in the furnace is not pleasant, but if you have come through such an experience you can rejoice that your faith is genuine and that you are growing into maturity.

Finally, an encouragement. Both our readings – from *The Pilgrim's Progress* and from 1 Peter – urge us to look forward. When we reach the Celestial City there will be even greater rejoicing and even greater reward. Notice how the two readings each use this wonderful future hope to encourage us to live well now. Keeping our eyes on the 'prize' is what motivates and strengthens us to keep going in the present, whatever battles we face. If we know the glory that awaits us, the less we are likely to drop out; if we keep focused on our ultimate goal, we can keep trials in their proper perspective. May God fill us with 'inexpressible and glorious joy' as we continue our Christian pilgrimage, knowing that the best is yet to be.

TO PONDER …

How will keeping your eyes fixed on your future 'prize' help you in the particular challenges you face at the moment?

PRAYER

Father, thank You for seeing me through many difficulties in my life so far. I have been weak but You are strong. I praise You that You have sustained me. Help me to see trials in their proper light, and to keep going when things are difficult. Most of all I praise You for the sure and certain hope that all those with genuine faith have. Thank You that You are faithful to Your promise to save all those who come to You. Fill me with great joy as I reflect on these things. Amen.

DAY 18

Faith under fire

Acts 14:22; 2 Timothy 3:12

Christian and Faithful respect Evangelist for his spiritual maturity, wisdom and guidance. They see he has gifts of prophecy and so ask him to tell them more of what to expect on their journey. They understand now there will be challenges ahead, so ask his advice on how best 'to resist and overcome them'. Evangelist is able to prepare the two pilgrims for the challenges that await them.

EVANGELIST: My sons, you have heard in the word of the truth of the gospel, that you must, through many tribulations, enter into the kingdom of heaven. And again, that in every city, bonds and afflictions abide in you; and therefore you cannot expect that you should go long on your pilgrimage without them, in some sort or other. You have found something of the truth of these testimonies upon you already, and more will immediately follow; for now, as you see, you are almost out of this wilderness, and therefore you will soon come into a town that you will by and by see before you; and in that town you will be hardly beset with enemies, who will strain hard but they will kill you; and be you sure that one or both of you must seal the testimony which you hold, with blood; but be you faithful unto death, and the King will give you a crown of life.

When John Bunyan wrote about persecution, he knew what it was like from personal experience. Imprisoned twice by the authorities for preaching the gospel, he had to endure squalid conditions and separation from his beloved family, who were left to wonder how they would live day to day. Even when he wasn't locked up, the threat of imprisonment – or worse – was often very real. Like the pilgrims he writes about, he could easily have lost his life because of the gospel. Bunyan lived in dangerous times.

State-sponsored persecution is also a reality for many Christians around the world today. As we reflect on this theme, one of the actions we can take is to pray for them, and find other ways to support them in their struggle (see the 'to ponder' section below for further suggestions).

In the West, we are very privileged: we don't suffer persecution of this sort. How many of us have been locked up in a dark, damp, dirty jail for many years because of our faith? And how many of us fear for our lives? Nevertheless, whilst we need to keep things in perspective, it's not easy to live as a Christian in contemporary Britain. Many workplaces are difficult contexts in which to live out our faith, and it can be tough in many homes too. A lot of courage, wisdom, and strength is needed to stay faithful in these situations. 2 Timothy 3:12 reminds us that if we are living godly, Christian lives we will be persecuted. Does this sound discouraging? Rather, it should encourage us. We are not alone, for many Christians have walked the path of persecution before us, and if we are suffering persecution it is evidence we are living godly lives, 'in Christ Jesus'. So take heart and continue to be faithful.

Notice that Evangelist refers to 'many tribulations'. We don't only suffer persecution; we suffer in other ways too. Such hardships are inevitable, for we live in a broken, hurting, fallen world. This is a place which, although still beautiful, has been damaged by human sin. There is suffering. But one of the important messages of *The Pilgrim's Progress* is that hardships are not just inevitable – God uses them to grow Christian maturity in us. This theme has already surfaced in some of our reflections, not least in yesterday's. Evangelist wanted to prepare Christian and Faithful for future suffering. Perhaps God wants to prepare you for some hardships that will be ahead for you. If so, don't be afraid. He will be with you, by the Holy Spirit, every step of the way. And as you go through trials you will be entering into the fullness of God's kingdom.

TO PONDER ...

Why not pray for the persecuted Church, not just today but on a more regular basis? You could focus on one country, or one region of the world so you can pray in greater depth. Organisations such as Christian Solidarity Worldwide and Open Doors can provide helpful information and facilitate your prayers.

PRAYER

Father, I lift before You the persecuted Church around the world. Protect them and strengthen them by the Spirit. Comfort them, encourage them, and reassure them of their heavenly reward. Help me to be ready for suffering when it comes and remain 'true to the faith'. Amen.

Wisdom

Proverbs 3:13–26; 23:23; James 1:5

Evangelist's warning is a terrible one but Christian and Faithful are not put off. They find themselves in the Town of Vanity, which holds a fair all year round by the name of Vanity Fair. This Fair sells all sorts of merchandise and offers all kinds of entertainment. The Lord of the Fair is Beelzebub, and Vanity's townsfolk are citizens of his kingdom. They do not like the two pilgrims, who show no interest in their 'vanities', but who instead insist that they 'buy the truth' only and have no care for what they see around them. The townsfolk despise all talk of the heavenly city and try and tempt them to buy from the Fair. The pilgrims refuse to listen. Instead, they look up towards heaven.

> *One chanced mockingly, beholding the carriages of the men to say unto them, What will ye buy? But they, looking gravely upon him, said, 'We buy the truth.' At that, there was an occasion taken to despise the men the more; some mocking, some taunting, some speaking reproachfully, and some calling upon others to smite them.*

'We buy the truth.' That's a powerful phrase! It actually comes direct from God's Word, from our Bible reading for today, Proverbs 23:23. The truth referred to is God's Word, as we might expect. But, tellingly, the verse encourages us to apply Scripture, to grow in 'understanding' and 'wisdom'. It's one thing to have God's Word, another to know it well, and still another to be able to think biblically about a range of situations and challenges we may face. As we grow in understanding of God's Word – of the unfolding biblical story as well as individual verses – then we will be able to bring the Scriptures to bear on the wide range of complex problems we have to face in the twenty-first century world.

Notice one thing about the pilgrims. They keep a commitment to the truth in the midst of great pressure. They are mocked because of their 'carriages' – meaning the godly and gracious way they behave or 'carry themselves'. But despite this mockery, their resolve to only buy the 'truth' remains.

When they get into even more difficulty, with the threat of physical violence, still they do not falter. It's easier to act with godly wisdom when we are commended for it; it's not so easy when we get into trouble for faithful and wise living. Bunyan knew what it was like to suffer for doing God's will. He was like Christian and Faithful: persecuted for his faith but still committed to God and His ways.

May Jesus, the living Word, the one who personifies wisdom, strengthen us by the Holy Spirit to grow in knowledge and wisdom. And may He help us to apply it in all circumstances, whatever the cost.

TO PONDER ...

In what area do you most need to know the wisdom of God today? It may be in a particular area of your personal life, or perhaps a pending decision, or a situation you're not sure how to respond to. Ask God now for wisdom, remembering the words of James 1:5: 'If any of you lacks wisdom, you should ask God, who gives generously to all without finding fault, and it will be given to you.'

PRAYER

Dear Lord, help me to grow in understanding of Your Word, and strengthen me to apply it to my life day by day, with godly wisdom. Help me to become all You want me to be, and respond in the ways You want me to respond. Give me the wisdom to know Your will, and the courage to do it. Amen.

DAY 20

Faithful unto death

Acts 7:54–60; Romans 8:38–39; Revelation 2:10

So the two pilgrims are brought to trial by a town that has very little but hatred for them. Their judge is called Lord Hate-good. Christian and Faithful are reminded of Evangelist's words and comfort one another, reassured that they are in the hands of a sovereign God.

The trial commences. Faithful is the first to speak and the first to be tried. He speaks boldly of his faith and is unafraid to challenge the jury. Showing utter contempt for the 'faithful' pilgrim, the jury unanimously conclude that he is guilty and sentence him to 'the most cruel death that could be invented'.

They, therefore, brought him out, to do with him according to their law; and, first, they scourged him, then they buffeted him, then they lanced his flesh with knives; after that they stoned him with stones, then pricked him with their swords; and, last of all, they burned him to ashes at the stake. Thus came Faithful to his end.

Now I saw that there stood behind the multitude, a chariot and a couple of horses, waiting for Faithful, who (so soon as his adversaries had despatched him) was taken up into it, and straightway was carried up through the clouds, with sound of trumpet, the nearest way to the Celestial Gate.

But as for Christian, he had some respite, and was remanded back to prison. So he there remained for a space; but he that overrules all things, having the power of their rage in his own hand, so wrought it about, that Christian for that time escaped them, and went his way.

In this moving passage from *The Pilgrim's Progress*, Christian is saved by God – 'he that overrules all things' – from a terrible death. Following a mockery of a trial, Faithful is cruelly killed. Yet Christian is only sent back to prison and, after a while, he escapes (we are not told how) and carries on his pilgrimage. Many Christians have their own wonderful stories of deliverance to tell. Bunyan, for all he suffered, was one of them. Although he was unfairly imprisoned, at least he wasn't deported from the country or killed, as he easily might have been. Eventually he was released. Perhaps you have been in a really tough situation. There seemed no way of escape and you felt trapped and afraid. But God rescued you; He turned the situation around. Thank God for what He did for you.

God delivered Christian, and God delivered Faithful too. Does that seem a strange thing to say? Didn't Faithful's persecution end in torture and death? Yes it did, and in many ways it was a terrible tragedy. Yet God was with him. Faithful didn't choose to die, but in this awful situation God strengthened him so that he didn't deny his Lord. Thanks to the power of the Holy Spirit, his end was peaceful and a real witness to those around him. And God's deliverance of Faithful was still more wonderful. Chariots and horses carried him 'straightway' to the Celestial City where he received (as it says in Revelation) the crown of life – a crown promised to all who remain 'faithful' to the end. God delivered Faithful just as surely as He delivered Christian.

In our reading from Acts 7, we see a striking, biblical example of God's deliverance. Stephen is stoned to death, the first person ever to be killed for following Jesus. There are some clear similarities between his story and Faithful's. Stephen knows God's presence and help, and like Faithful he is a wonderful witness to the love of Christ in his heart. His death mirrors Faithful's in that it too is remarkably peaceful: the original Greek of Acts 7:60 literally says he 'fell asleep'. And Stephen too was welcomed by Jesus into heaven (see Acts 7:55). In Stephen's life and death, we see the God who saves in action. That God can save in spite of death should not surprise us. Jesus is risen! He has conquered the grave. We have proof He is able to bring us through death, and we know He will do this because He loves us. We can trust Him. Faithful and Stephen show us a powerful truth. Our greatest fear, death itself, will not separate us from God's wonderful love.

What is your greatest fear? It may well be death. If so, be sure that Jesus has conquered it. He will bring you through this, and He can bring you through anything. *Nothing* can separate us from God's love for us in Christ (Romans 8:38–39)! Knowing this strengthens us to face our fears with renewed faith and courage. We too can be 'faithful' because we are loved by such a faithful God.

TO PONDER …

Realising that death has been defeated gives us great courage as Christians, and helps us pass from fear to faith. Ask yourself again, what is your biggest fear? Give it to Jesus and ask for His help to overcome it. Because of Jesus' resurrection, even death does not have the last word for us. The last word is resurrection! He promises us life, and life for evermore. We can face the present – and the future – with confidence.

PRAYER

Father, thank You that Jesus has conquered death. Thank You that He has the power to deliver us and that, because of His great love for us, He does this again and again. Thank You for the ways He has delivered me in the past. Thank You that even in death He will deliver me. Help me not to be afraid, but to trust in You. Amen.

A new disciple

To the Glory of God and in memory of John Rowan Steven who was drowned in the River Ouse on June 15th 1927 while trying to save his friend.

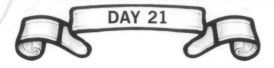

Bearing witness

Acts 16:25–34

So we are told that 'he that over-rules all things' enables Christian to escape from Vanity Fair and continue on his way. He is alone on the journey now. He has lost a dear and faithful companion, but Christian is not downhearted. He knows that Faithful is with his Saviour in heaven and in this Faithful has the victory.

Safe in this knowledge, Christian goes on his way, singing and praising God. But he is not alone for long. God knows his need and soon provides him with a new companion.

Now I saw in my dream, that Christian went not forth alone, for there was one whose name was Hopeful (being so made by the beholding of Christian and Faithful in their words and behaviour, in their sufferings at the Fair) who joined himself unto him, and, entering into a brotherly covenant, told him that he would be his companion. Thus, one died to bear testimony to the truth, and another rises out of his ashes, to be a companion with Christian in his pilgrimage. This Hopeful also told Christian, that there were many more of the men in the Fair, that would take their time and follow after.

Was the terrible suffering experienced by Christian, and especially Faithful, all for nothing? No, because at least one inhabitant of Vanity Fair has been changed by their witness. Christian's gracious, God-honouring 'words and behaviour', when they were under great pressure, have made someone 'hopeful' of a better life. And so Hopeful joins Christian on his pilgrimage. We will read his testimony later in the story, but by his name Bunyan shows us that here is a man who has experienced true conversion. Encouragingly, Hopeful tells Christian that many others are likely to follow in time.

With a pastor's skill, Bunyan makes two really important points. First, God provides Christian with exactly what he needs: a new companion for his journey. Christian has really struggled when he has been on his own, or when he has had unhelpful companions. He needs a good Christian friend to support him and so God graciously provides just the right person. What is your need right now? It may be exactly the same as Bunyan's pilgrim, a strong Christian friend who you can 'travel' with and be accountable to. Or perhaps there is a different but equally pressing need? Bring it to God in prayer today. It is important to remember He provides for our needs, not our wants. Also, He doesn't always respond to our requests in the way we expect! Nevertheless, He loves us, knows what we need, and provides for us. Don't be afraid to ask God, and don't forget to look out for the answer so you can thank Him when it comes.

Bunyan's second point is about our witness, and it's at the heart of our passage today. Christian and Faithful's godly behaviour and words seemed to have achieved nothing: one of them died, the other had to flee the town. But in fact, a man was converted, with many more challenged. In our Bible reading, Paul and Silas' joyful response to suffering and unjust imprisonment is to praise God and then lovingly share with the very man who had locked them up. It made a wonderful difference, not only to the jailer, but to his whole family. Why were Paul and Silas so joyful and why hadn't they escaped when they had the chance? What was it that these men had that made them so different? No wonder the man was ready to hear the gospel, and to respond. God uses our witness, and He often especially uses our witness in pressure situations. Do we have a faith that carries us through great trials? Do we have a commitment to God that means we do the right and godly things even when the heat is on? If so, people invariably sit up and take notice. Faithfulness under fire makes a great difference. Pray that God will help you to develop such faithfulness, and that God would use this to bring others to Jesus.

TO PONDER …

What are the pressure situations that you face? How can you be faithful to God at such times?

PRAYER

Lord, thank You that You provide for me. I bring my particular need to You. Answer my prayer, not in my way, but in Your way. Continue to provide for me, Lord. Help me to be a faithful witness under fire. And just as You do in the story of Paul and Silas, make that faithful witness fruitful. Amen.

Refreshment and renewal

Psalm 46; Ephesians 5:18

Christian and his new companion Hopeful journey on together, meeting many characters along the way, the first of which is Mr By-ends of the Town of Fair Speech, a friend of Mr Money-love, Mr Hold-the-world and Mr Save-all. These men do not uphold the same beliefs as Christian and Hopeful and they soon part company. The pilgrims then come to an old monument of a woman transformed into a pillar. This is to remind pilgrims of the story of Lot's wife, how she was delivered from one judgment only to be destroyed by another. Christian and Hopeful perceive this monument to be both a 'caution' and an 'example' and determine 'always to remember Lot's wife'.

I saw, then, that they went on their way to a pleasant river; which David the king called 'the river of God', but John 'the river of the water of life'. Now their way lay just upon the bank of the river; here, therefore, Christian and his companion walked with great delight; they drank also of the water of the river, which was pleasant, and enlivening to their weary spirits: besides, on the banks of this river, on either side, were green trees, that bore all manner of fruit; and the leaves of the trees were good for medicine; with the fruit of these trees they were also much delighted; and the leaves they eat to prevent surfeits, and other diseases that are incident to those that heat their blood by travels. On either side of the river was also a meadow, curiously beautified with lilies, and it was green all the year long. In this meadow they lay down, and slept; for here they might lie down safely. When they awoke, they gathered again of the fruit of the trees, and drank again of the water of the river, and then lay down again to sleep. Thus they did several days and nights.

In yesterday's reflection, part of the focus was on the God who provides. Here we see this truth highlighted again. Bunyan skilfully paints a beautiful picture. The bone-weary pilgrims come to a place where there are green trees heavy with fruit to eat and with leaves that bring healing. There is a meadow, lush and green not just in the spring and summer but 'all the year long'. And in the centre of this scene there is a river. It is this river that brings life to everything else; it makes the trees grow and the meadow flourish. Water is essential for the traveller. Without it, someone on a long and difficult journey will soon die. Here pilgrims can stop and drink as much water as they need. Here is rest, refreshment and renewal.

Bunyan had understood something crucial about the Christian life. We cannot survive, let alone thrive, without the refreshing and renewal that God gives us. How do we get this? Biblically, a river, or water, is a symbol for the Holy Spirit. We are encouraged to come to God and 'be filled' with the Holy Spirit (Ephesians 5:18). We might actually translate Paul's words in Ephesians to 'be *being* filled', for it is the present continuous tense that is used. We can come to God daily and ask to be filled. He promises us the 'living water' of the Spirit. So don't be afraid to drink deeply.

God also refreshes us through his Word, the Bible. Through it He teaches us, nourishes us, shapes us and challenges us. His Word is life and health and peace. So we need both Word and Spirit, in fact the two go together. Sometimes Christians who study the Bible intently become very dry and dusty. They need the water of the Spirit to flow into them and refresh them. And sometimes Christians talk about being filled with the Spirit, but it's all froth and bubble. There is little substance, and when suffering comes, they soon give up. We need both Word and Spirit.

It's good to take time out of our daily routines to spend it with God. Christian and Hopeful were resting by the river for a number of days. If you can take a period of time to go on retreat, to spend quality and quantity time with God, then do so. But spending some time with God every day is foundational. This is not always easy to do with our fast-paced and complex lives. But it is a huge help to us on our journey. God longs to give us all we need by His Word and through His Spirit. Every day He gives us the invitation, come and drink, come and feast, come and live.

TO PONDER ...

Do you spend time with God daily? How can you grow, maintain and further develop this good and godly habit? Don't feel defeated if you're struggling with this. We all struggle with it at different times. But don't give up. Determine to drink more of the living water and feed more at God's glorious feast.

PRAYER

Read Psalm 46 again. In the quietness and stillness, use the words to help you pray today.

Wandering from the path

Romans 8:28; 1 Corinthians 10:12,13

Christian and Hopeful spend some time at the river of the water of life, eating the fruit of the trees and drinking from the river. Refreshed and ready to go on, they follow the river until it comes to an end. But the road becomes rough and difficult. Wishing for a better way, they spy a stile leading to By-path Meadow. Christian is keen to follow the path through the meadow as it looks easier than the path ahead of them. Hopeful is unsure, worried that the path will lead them out of the way, but allows Christian to persuade him. The path is easy and they are soon joined by a fellow pilgrim, Vain-confidence. As his name suggests, he confidently assures the two pilgrims that they are indeed on the road to the Celestial City. Vain-confidence marches on in his own strength but when night comes, unable to see where he is going, he falls into a deep pit and is dashed to pieces.

Now, Christian and his fellow heard him fall. So they called to know the matter, but there was none to answer; only they heard a groaning. Then said Hopeful, Where are we now? Then was his fellow silent, as mistrusting that he had led him out of the way; and now it began to rain, and thunder, and lighten in a very dreadful manner; and the water rose amain [suddenly].

Then Hopeful groaned in himself, saying, Oh that I had kept on my way!

CHRISTIAN: Who could have thought that this path should have led us out of the way?

HOPEFUL: I was afraid on it at the very first, and therefore gave you that gentle caution. I would have spoke plainer, but that you are older than I.

CHRISTIAN: Good Brother, be not offended; I am sorry I have brought thee out of the way, and that I have put thee into such imminent danger; pray, my brother, forgive me; I did not do it of an evil intent.

HOPEFUL: Be comforted, my brother, for I forgive thee; and believe too that this shall be for our good.

Things have been going well, but now disaster strikes! Surprisingly, it is Christian who leads Hopeful, still a relatively new believer, astray. By this stage, Christian has grown in maturity, but he still wanders from the path, taking his younger companion with him. We may have made great progress in the Christian life, but we can still make big mistakes that have serious consequences for us and for others. We should never be complacent, and always guard against pride creeping into our lives. Many Christians who were thought 'mature' have fallen badly, including many Christian leaders. We need to hear Paul's words in 1 Corinthians 10:12: 'if you think you are standing firm, be careful that you don't fall!'

Why did Christian make this mistake? It was because the right way was the hard way. Therefore, he did not want to take it. Here is a challenge for us too. Ask God for the character and strength to choose the right path, whether that path is smooth and easy or, as it often is, narrow and difficult. Wandering from the path will have real consequences, as we shall see. Sin matters. As we explored right at the beginning of our journey, sin is rebellion against God. It messes up our lives and will affect the lives of others. It always spells danger. Our passage from *The Pilgrim's Progress* acts as a warning for us today.

Nevertheless, although Christian and Hopeful faced disaster, they did not need to despair. God was with them and was still working, as Hopeful recognised. He forgives his friend and reassures him that God is in control. This is the truth of Romans 8:28. Notice that the verse does not say that everything that happens *is* good. But God is able to *bring* good out of our wrong turns and stumbles. Most importantly, He is more than able to bring us back onto the right path. If you have wandered away from God, or are in the process of wandering away, this is a strong challenge for you today. But you can be reassured that however far you've travelled, God wants to call you back, and He can do it. We cannot wander out of the reach of God. This is yet one more facet of His glorious grace.

TO PONDER …

Are you in danger of 'wandering from the path' in an area of your life? Now is the time to repent and turn back. Talk to God today.

PRAYER

Lord, thank You for the challenge You set me to continue strongly in the Christian life, keeping on the right paths. Help me to discern how You are calling me to live and please give me the strength and encouragement to live according to Your Word. Thank You that when I do wander, I never go beyond the reach of Your grace. Forgive me I pray, and lead me back. Amen.

Endurance

CHRISTIAN · VANQUISHES · THE · FIEND · APOLLYON

more than conquerors through Him that loved us · Romans VIII 37 · we are things these in all Nay

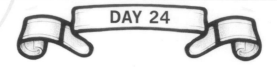

God's sovereignty

James 4:8; 1 Peter 1:3–7

Unfortunately for the pilgrims, they have trespassed onto the grounds of Doubting Castle, owned by Giant Despair and his wife Diffidence. Walking early in his grounds, the giant finds the two pilgrims and forces them to go with him to his castle, where he throws them into 'a very dark dungeon, nasty and stinking to the spirit of these two men'. Christian and Hopeful are desperate, particularly Christian who blames himself for the trouble they now find themselves in. Giant Despair and his wife are determined to see the pilgrims die. Although he is the more mature pilgrim, Christian has little strength left and contemplates ending his life – exactly what his captors are encouraging. Hopeful however, despite the terrible situation they are in, reminds Christian of the hope they have in the 'God that made the world' and encourages his weaker brother with much exhortation and reminders of 'former things'.

> HOPEFUL: *My Brother, said he, rememberest thou not how valiant thou hast been heretofore? Apollyon could not crush thee, nor could all that thou didst hear, or see, or feel in the Valley of the Shadow of Death. What hardship, terror, and amazement hast thou already gone through! And art thou now nothing but fear! Thou seest that I am in the dungeon with thee, a far weaker man by nature than thou art; also, this Giant has wounded me as well as thee; and hath also cut off the bread and water from my mouth; and with thee I mourn without the light. But let us exercise a little more patience; remember how thou playedst the man at Vanity Fair, and wast neither afraid of the chain, nor cage, nor yet of*

bloody death. Wherefore let us (at least to avoid the shame, that becomes not a Christian to be found in) bear up with patience as well as we can.

Christian and Hopeful have made a terrible mistake. What Christian thought was a harmless detour has turned into the most desperate and dangerous experience. They are trapped in a dark and dingy dungeon with what appears to be little hope of escape. Giant Despair and his wife are determined the pilgrims will end their lives at Doubting Castle. Christian and Hopeful are in an extreme situation.

When we feel trapped in a difficult situation we can easily become disillusioned, hopeless, faithless and despairing. We can feel completely alone even when we are not. And, perhaps most terrible of all, God can also feel remote and distant. We must do all we can to avoid the mistake that Christian and Hopeful make in straying off the 'narrow way' and into an encounter with 'Giant Despair'. But if we have strayed, today's reading encourages us to draw near to God, and as we do, He will draw near to us.

But, even the strongest and mature Christians will experience times of difficulty and despair. The Bible teaches us to expect this; it is part of discipleship. But the Bible also shows us that, at all times and in all circumstances, God is still sovereign. We need to keep this promise close to us at all times. Our God is a faithful God. He will never leave us nor forsake us. As we learnt yesterday, even in our mistakes, our wrong turns or our suffering, God is in control and He will work everything for our good.

TO PONDER …

Think about a time when you took the wrong path. Where did it lead you? What happened and what did you learn from it? Make a mental or written note of the lessons you have learnt from this experience, and thank God for them. Our wrong turns are never right, but God can be so creative with them that as we look back, they can even begin to appear right!

PRAYER

Father, I thank You for Your amazing promises. Thank You for caring for every detail of my life. I'm sorry for the mistakes I make. Thank You for teaching me through them and for working them for my good. Strengthen me on my journey and help me to stay on the narrow way, even when other ways seem easier and more attractive. And help me to be a source of strength to my fellow pilgrims. Amen.

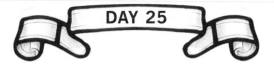

God's promises

Acts 12:6–11; 2 Corinthians 1:20; Matthew 6:26

When Giant Despair and his wife Diffidence realise that the pilgrims are refusing to take their own lives, they devise another plan to cause them even greater despair and take away their hope. The giant takes the pilgrims to the castle-yard and shows them the bones and skulls of all the pilgrims that he and his wife had torn to pieces. This, the giant warns them, is what he will do to them.

But Giant Despair and Diffidence have a nagging doubt that the pilgrims may not have yet given up all hope. The giant resolves to search the pilgrims to check they are not hiding anything that will help them escape but, already in bed and wanting his sleep, he decides it can wait until morning.

Well, on Saturday, about midnight, they began to pray, and continued in prayer till almost break of day.

Now, a little before it was day, good Christian, as one half amazed, brake out in this passionate speech: What a fool, quoth [said] he, am I, thus to lie in a stinking dungeon, when I may as well walk at liberty? I have a key, called Promise, that will, I am persuaded, open any lock in Doubting Castle. Then said Hopeful, That is good news, good brother; pluck it and try. Then Christian began to try at the dungeon door, whose bolt (as he turned the key) gave back, and the door flew open with ease, and Christian and Hopeful both came out. Then he went to the outward door that leads into the castle-yard, and, with his key, opened that door also. After, he went to the iron gate, for that must be opened too;

but that lock went damnable hard, yet the key did open it. Then they thrust open the gate to make their escape with speed, but that gate, as it opened, made such a creaking, that it waked Giant Despair, who hastily rising to pursue his prisoners, felt his limbs to fail, for his fits took him again, so that he could by no means go after them. Then they went on, and came to the King's highway again, and so were safe, because they were out of his jurisdiction.

Free at last! Dramatically, the pilgrims make their escape. Bunyan tells the story with great skill. Door by door the key gets them through. But what about the iron gate? It's stiff and to begin with the key will not turn. Perhaps they are trapped after all. Yet the key is turned again and this time the lock shifts and turns, although with agonising slowness. The pilgrims push hard at the heavy gate. The giant begins to pursue but ends up lumbering clumsily after them. Perhaps his power was never so great after all. The pilgrims reach the King's highway – safety! Giant Despair is still alive and real. But now they are out of his reach.

What is the secret of Christian and Hopeful's escape? The key, yes; but what does the key signify? Bunyan tells us that the key stands for promise, more specifically, the promises of God. The Bible is full of God's promises: estimates vary but there is common agreement there are over three thousand. Whatever your situation, even if you are in a 'Doubting Castle' of your own, there is a promise that can act like a key: it can set you free. How does this work? To begin with you need to know the key is there. Christian had the key all along, but he'd forgotten. Then you need to use it. In other words, believe the promise. Believe that what God says is true. Trust that every promise is fulfilled in Jesus, as our Bible verse from 2 Corinthians reminds us. Ask God to apply His promises to your heart by the Holy Spirit. Use the promise as your key to freedom.

An example can help us grasp this more clearly. Assume someone feels they are worthless. They may have been told this by people around them, maybe even family members. They may have experienced things that have caused shame and hurt. Or perhaps they have a poor self-image and self-worth because of the messages that are all around us, that we need to look a certain way or be able to buy certain things to have value. But all these messages are lies. Listen to the truth of God: we are immensely valuable to him (Matthew 6:26). Know 'without a doubt' (as Peter did in Acts 12) that God loves us and will care for us.

Know His promises, believe His promises. They will open doors to freedom.

TO PONDER ...
What are your struggles? What promises of God do you need to cling to, and truly believe in?

PRAYER
Lord, thank You that Your promises are keys that unlock the doors leading from fear to freedom. Thank You that I can trust Your promises. Even reliable people can let us down, but You are always faithful. You always deliver, at just the right time. Increase my faith in You, my faithful God. Amen.

God's faithfulness

Hebrews 11:1; Deuteronomy 32:4

The pilgrims, sustained by the promises of God, escape the land of Giant Despair and Doubting Castle, crossing over the stile through which they had entered the Meadow. But, wanting to share their knowledge and experience with future pilgrims, they stop to erect a pillar on which they engrave words of warning.

Continuing along the King's highway, the pilgrims meet with 'a very brisk lad' by the name of Ignorance, from the 'country of Conceit'. They determine, from talking with him briefly, that he is not a true pilgrim and discern this is not the right time to get into conversation with him. So they continue on without him.

Christian is soon reminded of a story that he relates to Hopeful. It is the story of a good man, Little-faith, who lives in the Town of Sincere. Little-faith is set upon by three brothers – Mistrust, Faint-heart and Guilt. He survives the attack, but only just. Christian uses this tale to teach Hopeful a lesson: where 'faithless' pilgrims would give up and sell what little they have, pilgrims 'that have faith, saving faith, though but a little of it' will hold on to it. There are pilgrims with 'Great-grace' and there are pilgrims with 'Little-faith'.

CHRISTIAN: True, they have often fled, both they and their master, when Great-grace hath but appeared; and no marvel; for he is the King's Champion. But, I trow [believe], you will put some difference betwixt Little-faith and the King's Champion. All the King's subjects are not his champions, nor can they, when tried, do such feats of war as he. Is it meet to think that a little child should handle Goliah as David did? Or that there should be the strength of an ox in a wren? Some are strong, some are weak; some have great faith, some have little. This man was one of the weak, and therefore he went to the wall.

Faith is absolutely crucial to the Christian life, as our Bible reading today so powerfully demonstrates. Bunyan has some important things to say about it. The challenge is to have great faith, and with real insight he shows us the way our faith grows. First, if we truly appreciate the 'great grace' we have received, then we will have great faith. If we realise we are deeply loved by God, then we will know we can trust Him. It is those who know they have received much grace who will be able to ride into battle as the 'King's Champion', trusting that God will ride out with them. Second, our faith grows through being tested. David's faith was tested in the battle with Goliath, but as he trusted God, so he was victorious and gained strength and confidence for other battles to come. Faith is like a muscle, the harder it works, the stronger it becomes.

But what about Little-faith? He doesn't seem a promising character, but it's important we notice how lovingly Bunyan depicts him. When Christian says he 'went to the wall', he doesn't mean Little-faith was lost, that somehow he wasn't a true believer after all. *The Pilgrim's Progress* is very clear that Little faith still had 'saving faith'. With a pastor's heart, Bunyan assures us that even if we have a small amount of saving faith it will be enough. There are times when we stumble and fall in the Christian life but God picks us up again. There are times when we struggle with doubt but God is merciful to us.

This brings us to the real heart of the passage, not great faith nor 'little faith' but God's faithfulness. Whatever the 'amount' of our faith, if it's true saving faith, then God will see us through. How did David defeat the giant Goliath when the odds were stacked against him and the situation was so terrifying? Was it because of his faith? Partly, but more importantly it was because God was with him and was faithful! The real hero of the story of David and Goliath is not the young man who strode into battle with his sling and five smooth stones. The real hero is God Himself. So it is with *The Pilgrim's Progress*. Yes, the faith of Christian and his fellow pilgrims is important, but at the heart of the story is a wonderful, loving, faithful God. God calls us to grow in faith. But even if we have 'little faith', we can rejoice. Whatever our struggles, God remains the same. He is always faithful.

TO PONDER ...

Is your faith being tested and stretched at the moment? Or can you remember a recent time when it was? If you have time, read the whole of Hebrews 11. It is a wonderfully inspiring passage. Take a moment to reflect on how God has shown His love to you in the past. As you do so, allow your faith in His goodness and care to be rekindled and fanned into flame.

PRAYER

Lord, please help me to grow in faith as I appreciate, more and more, all You do for me. You are a trustworthy, gracious God. Be with those I know who are finding trusting You tough at the moment. Work by the power of the Spirit in their lives, and strengthen me too I pray. Amen.

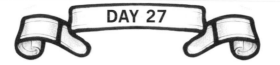

Walk by faith, not by sight

2 Corinthians 5:7; 1 Peter 3:15; Proverbs 19:27

Christian and Hopeful press on in their journey, but despite their maturing faith, they soon fall into another trap. They meet the Flatterer, a false apostle, who lures the pilgrims onto the wrong path by his smooth speech. He soon has the two pilgrims entwined in his net. An angel appears to rescue them but, before doing so, admonishes and punishes them, reminding the pilgrims of another of God's promises: 'As many as I love, I rebuke and chasten; be zealous, therefore, and repent.' The pilgrims understand that discipline is from God and for the good of pilgrims, so they thank the angel for all his kindness and continue on their way singing – a reminder that joy should accompany our Christian journey through good times and hard.

Next they meet a man called Atheist. After a short and futile conversation with him, Christian and Hopeful determine that they should learn the lesson of their previous encounter and walk on.

Then said Christian to Hopeful his fellow, Is it true which this man hath said?

HOPEFUL: Take heed, he is one of the flatterers; remember what it cost us once already for our hearkening to such kind of fellows. What! No Mount Zion? Did we not see, from the Delectable Mountains the gate of the city? Also, are we not now to walk by faith? Let us go on, said Hopeful, lest the man with the whip overtake us again. You should have taught me that lesson, which I will round you in the ears withal: 'Cease, my son, to hear the instruction THAT CAUSETH to err from the words of knowledge'.

I say, my brother, cease to hear him, and let us 'believe to the saving of the soul.'

CHRISTIAN: My brother, I did not put the question to thee, for that I doubted of the truth of our belief myself, but to prove thee, and to fetch from thee a fruit of the honesty of thy heart. As for this man, I know that he is blinded by the god of this world. Let thee and I go on, knowing that we have belief of the truth, 'and no lie is of the truth'.

HOPEFUL: Now do I rejoice in hope of the glory of God.

So they turned away from the man; and he, laughing at them, went his way.

Christian and Hopeful's encounter with Atheist is a brief one, mainly because they have learnt some hard lessons along the way already and do not want to make another mistake. But this is also perhaps reflective of the challenges of Bunyan's day. The battles Bunyan and his fellow Christians had were not so much with atheists. Belief in God, even if this belief was not central to their lives, was foundational for most people at that time. But we live in a world very different to Bunyan's. If he were writing *The Pilgrim's Progress* today, the character Atheist may well be more prominent.

How do the pilgrims respond to Atheist? The first thing to note is that they do talk with him. They ask him where he is going and spend a few moments in conversation. But while they politely question him regarding his beliefs, they do not allow him to distract them from their own journey nor do they weaken in their position of faith. They speak with conviction. And when they realise that his mind is made up, they decide to walk on. There are two simple but important lessons here for us as Christians. We must not ignore the debate; but neither must we get sidetracked by it.

But we can take more from this passage. We are reminded by both Christian and Hopeful of the importance of God's Word. Hopeful tells us that we must cease to listen to anyone who causes us to drift from 'the words of knowledge'. God's Word is the ultimate knowledge we need as Christians to guide us on our journey. It is, as Christian says, the truth. The better our knowledge of God's Word, the closer we will keep to it and so to God. To 'know' the Bible is to 'know' more of God. This knowledge matures us spiritually and strengthens us for the Christian journey. It also impacts others. The more we know of God, the more prepared we will be 'to give an answer to everyone who asks [us] to give the reason for the hope that [we] have ... with gentleness and respect' (1 Peter 3:15). To be confident Christians, we must be knowledgeable Christians; and to be knowledgeable Christians we must know God's Word. Only in this way will we truly be able to 'walk by faith, not by sight'.

TO PONDER ...

How well do you know your Bible? Determine to know it better, in order that your own faith will be strengthened.

PRAYER

Lord, thank You for Your Word. Please help me to know it better. Come by the Spirit and make it alive to me, and strengthen my faith in You. Amen.

Faithful fellowship

FAITHFUL
HELPING CHRISTIAN

Two are better than one

Ecclesiastes 4:9–10; James 5:16–20

Christian and Hopeful leave Atheist and continue their journey until they come to the Enchanted Ground, a place whose air immediately makes them drowsy and desiring of sleep. Hopeful is keen to take a nap, telling Christian that 'sleep is sweet to the labouring man; we may be refreshed if we take a nap'. But Christian this time is the wiser of the two and persuades Hopeful not to sleep. Hopeful, realising his mistake, acknowledges the real and vital benefits of Christian companionship.

HOPEFUL: I acknowledge myself in a fault; and had I been here alone, I had by sleeping run the danger of death. I see it is true that the wise man saith, 'Two ARE better than one.' Hitherto hath thy company been my mercy, and thou shalt have a good reward for thy labour.

CHRISTIAN: Now, then, said Christian, to prevent drowsiness in this place, let us fall into good discourse.

HOPEFUL: With all my heart, said the other.

CHRISTIAN: Where shall we begin?

HOPEFUL: Where God began with us. But do you begin, if you please.

CHRISTIAN: I will sing you first this song:
When saints do sleepy grow, let them come hither,
And hear how these two pilgrims talk together:

Yea, let them learn of them, in any wise
Thus to keep open their drowsy, slumb'ring eyes.
Saints' fellowship, if it be manag'd well,
Keeps them awake, and then away from hell.

When Faithful died at Vanity Fair and was taken up to heaven, Christian was not just left in prison, he was left alone – or so he thought. But God had not deserted him. He gave Christian a means of escape and a new companion. God knew Christian's needs. And he knows ours. At times we may be called upon to walk alone, and at these times we need to be particularly strong in our faith, keeping close to God. But God knows that the Christian pilgrimage is hard and that fellowship and companionship is important. We need the closeness with fellow Christians that enables us to grow in depth of faith and maturity, those with whom we can study God's Word, pray and share stories of our own Christian pilgrimage. This may involve challenge as well as comfort; questions as well as affirmations.

Christian and Hopeful demonstrate this companionship. They have enjoyed times of ease and times of trial together. They have been hurt and misguided by others, and made their own mistakes. They have learnt to challenge and be challenged, and they have learnt to forgive, not just others but each other. Their friendship has indeed been tested.

In everything, they have both endeavoured to put God first. Even when they have gone wrong, it was always with the intention of doing right. Their mistakes have enabled them to grow in spiritual wisdom and understanding and have given them renewed determination to keep going and to keep on the right path. Christian and Hopeful have grown in faith both as individuals and together, and while their ultimate dependence is on God and God alone, they have also learnt to respect and appreciate each other.

True Christian friendship is something that we too should treasure. To have a friend who shares our faith and who encourages us in it, a friend who prays for us, challenges us and comforts us according to our physical, emotional and spiritual needs, a friend whose love and support remains steadfast and firm in good times and difficult –

that is a true friend. Such a friend may be constantly by our side, an ever present companion; or be quietly in the background, supporting, encouraging, praying and loving but from a distance. Whoever or wherever they are, we should recognise them, treasure them and thank God for them.

TO PONDER …

Hopeful comments that 'two are better than one' and that Christian's company has at times been his 'mercy'. Our readings today remind us of the importance of Christian friendship – for support, encouragement, prayer, even 'mercy'. What friendships have been a 'mercy' to you on your journey through life? What friendships do you value now? Could you do more to treasure them?

PRAYER

Thank You Father, for all my Christian companions. Help me to be a good friend to them too. And thank You for the best friend of all, Your Son, Jesus Christ. Amen.

Religion or relationship

John 3:16; 1 Peter 3:18

So, to keep themselves from getting drowsy and falling asleep, the two pilgrims decide to enjoy some spiritual conversation. This prevents them from succumbing to the sleepy air and provides encouragement for the journey ahead. As Hopeful is the younger Christian and a relatively new companion, Christian asks him about his conversion experience.

Hopeful describes how he first became aware of his own sinfulness through the witness of Faithful and Christian at Vanity Fair. At first, he says, he tried to shut his eyes to 'the light'. He enjoyed sin and did not want to change. He liked his 'old Companions' and did not want to leave them, but neither would God leave him. Wherever he went he was reminded of sin and the thought of sinning became 'double torment' to him. He describes how he tried to change his ways, to become a good religious person. But this, he found, was not enough. At last, he spoke to Faithful, asking him what he should do. Faithful told him again of Jesus Christ, the one who had never sinned and the only one who can justify us in the sight of God. Hopeful had heard this before but hadn't believed. Now, he says, he understood that even at our best we are never good enough for God. He was ready to listen.

CHRISTIAN: And did you ask him what man this was, and how you must be justified by him?

HOPEFUL: Yes, and he told me it was the Lord Jesus, that dwelleth on the right hand of the Most High. And thus, said he, you must be justified by him, even by trusting to what he hath done by himself in the days of his flesh, and suffered when he did hang on the tree. I asked him further, how that man's righteousness could be of that efficacy to justify another before God? And he told me he was the mighty God, and did what he did, and died the death also, not for himself, but for me; to whom his doings, and the worthiness of them, should be imputed, if I believed on him.

Hearing how someone came to believe in Jesus is a great joy. There are few things more exciting than hearing how Jesus turned someone's life around. When was the last time you shared your story of how you came to faith in Christ as Saviour?

Hopeful's 'testimony' is a really powerful one. He recognises his terrible sinfulness, but has a real struggle breaking free from his old ways. He tries religion and good works but these fail. This parallels Bunyan's own experience. Bunyan himself tried religion, going to church on a regular basis. He tried 'good works', even managing to stop his habit of swearing through the force of his will. But although he seemed clean on the outside, he knew that on the inside he wasn't right. Religion failed and his own efforts failed. In the end he had nowhere to go but Jesus: His grace, His cross, His salvation. It is through relationship with Him that salvation is found. This is the path Hopeful takes too.

Hopeful's testimony is lively and joyful but it is certainly not shallow. It contains deep theology. In particular, he describes how Jesus died on the cross as a substitute for our sins. He died in our place, 'the righteous for the unrighteous' (1 Peter 3:18). Jesus' righteousness is transferred to us when we put our faith in Him. We are free because He was punished in our place; we are clean because He bore our sin on the cross.

The gospel really is the only way sin and rebellion can be dealt with. Our own efforts fail and religion fails. Only God's grace, only the cross, only Jesus dying in our place makes the difference. Consider again the words of John 3:16: 'For God *so* loved the world that he gave his one and only Son, that whoever believes in him shall not perish but have eternal life' (emphasis added). May God give us a deeper appreciation of these things. This is the wonderful good news we have to believe and share. It is good news about a relationship rather than religion.

TO PONDER ...

When people look at you, do they see a religious person, or someone who has a living relationship with Jesus and is full of the Holy Spirit?

PRAYER

Lord, I recognise that religion cannot save, neither can our own good works. Only the 'good work' of Your Son on the cross can save us. Thank You that Jesus died in my place, bearing the punishment that was rightfully mine. I praise You that because of His death, You declare me righteous, clean, forgiven! I worship You for Your great love. Amen.

DAY 30

The Word of truth

Romans 5:6–8

Christian then asks Hopeful what he did next. Hopeful explains that he objected to believing for he considered himself unworthy of being saved. Christian enquires how Faithful had responded to this. Hopeful replies that Faithful told him to go to Christ and see, but that he had felt that this was 'presumption'. Once again, Faithful responds confidently to Hopeful's caution, assuring him that Hopeful was – as we all are – 'invited to come'.

HOPEFUL: Then he gave me a book of Jesus, his inditing, to encourage me the more freely to come; and he said, concerning that book, That every jot and tittle there of stood firmer than heaven and earth. Then I asked him, What I must do when I came; and he told me, I must entreat upon my knees, with all my heart and soul, the Father to reveal him to me. Then I asked him further, how I must make my supplication to him? And he said, Go, and thou shalt find him upon a mercy-seat, where he sits all the year long, to give pardon and forgiveness to them that come. I told him, that I knew not what to say when I came. And he bid me say to this effect, God be merciful to me a sinner, and make me to know and believe in Jesus Christ; for I see, that if his righteousness had not been, or I have not faith in that righteousness, I am utterly cast away. Lord, I have heard that thou art a merciful God, and hast ordained that thy Son Jesus Christ should be the Saviour of the world; and moreover, that thou art willing to bestow him upon such a poor sinner as I am (and I am a sinner indeed), Lord, take therefore this opportunity, and magnify thy grace in the salvation of my soul, through thy Son Jesus Christ. Amen.

Hopeful's continuing testimony highlights themes we have encountered before in *The Pilgrim's Progress*. All of them are wonderful, and all bear repetition. We see the encouragement to come to Christ 'freely' – the gospel invitation is for all. The vital importance of the Scriptures and of prayer are also here, and so is grace. This last theme should come as no surprise, for it has been present in nearly every reading: Bunyan's writing is saturated with the grace of God. That is because he lived it and breathed it personally. As in Hopeful's prayer, Bunyan's aim was to 'magnify' the grace of God. For him there was no higher theme.

Hopeful's experience and prayer show us God's great grace by setting it alongside our sinfulness and rebellion. We are not good enough on our own, and God (as Bunyan has shown so often) is holy. Imagine a great canyon with us on one side and God on the other. We are separated from God by a great chasm of sin. We have no hope ourselves of getting across. We have seen characters in *The Pilgrim's Progress* try all sorts of things to bridge the gap – good works, religion, fine words … but not one of them will go the distance. The yawning chasm remains.

Despite this great divide, we don't need to despair, because Jesus has come! In a prayer full of rich, deep theology, Hopeful unpacks what Jesus has done for us. Christ is the Saviour of the world. Our unrighteousness leaves us stranded on the wrong side of the canyon, but Jesus' righteousness gets us across. He did nothing wrong, and yet He died for us. Romans 5:6–8 reassures us that Jesus died for the 'ungodly' and for 'sinners', for those who are 'powerless'. In other words, He died for us! We can imagine the cross bridging the gap between us and God. Grace is truly wonderful. No wonder this was Bunyan's greatest theme.

TO PONDER …

What is your story of coming to Jesus? When you share your testimony, do you point to God's grace, as Hopeful did? And what about when we share what God is doing in our lives right now? Sometimes the stories we tell focus on ourselves rather than God and His mercy and grace. Do we concentrate on all the wonderful things we think we have done for Him, or do we talk about all the wonderful things He has done for us?

How could you emphasise God's grace as you share with others all He has done in your life?

PRAYER

Lord, Your Word is true – I was a sinner, and powerless to do anything about it. I was 'cast away' like Hopeful, like somebody drowning, like someone stranded on the wrong side of the canyon. I praise You for sending Jesus to bridge the gap for me. Lord, I depend on Your wonderful, extravagant grace. Like Bunyan, I pray that grace would be the theme I return to again and again. Amen.

God's love and ours

2 Corinthians 12:9; 1 Timothy 1:15; Hebrews 7:25

Hopeful explains to Christian that he prayed this prayer 'over, and over, and over', but God did not straightaway reveal His Son to him. He was tempted to give up but two things stopped him: the knowledge that only through the righteousness of Christ could he be saved; and the promise in the Bible that 'though it tarry, wait for it; because it will surely come, it will not tarry' (Habakkuk 2:3, KJV). Hopeful describes how he continued in prayer until the Son was revealed to him – a revelation that came not with his 'bodily eyes' but with the eyes of his 'understanding'.

This was the moment of Hopeful's conversion; the moment he became 'Christian'. It was, he says, on a day when he was feeling particularly sad and desperate – sad because of an acute awareness of his own sinfulness in the sight of God; desperate because he understood the personal consequences of it for his soul. But then, Hopeful explains, quite suddenly and unexpectedly he saw the Lord Jesus looking down on him from heaven, urging him to believe in Him and be saved. He had waited, and Christ had indeed come! His prayers had been answered! But Hopeful was still unsure. Would Christ really save such a wretch as he?

> But I replied, Lord, I am a great, a very great sinner. And he answered, 'My grace is sufficient for thee'. Then I said, But, Lord, what is believing? And then I saw from that saying, 'He that cometh to me shall never hunger, and he that believeth on me shall never thirst;' that believing and coming was all one; and that he that came, that is, ran out in his heart and affections after salvation by Christ, he indeed believed in Christ. Then the water

stood in mine eyes, and I asked further, But, Lord, may such a great sinner as I am, be indeed accepted of thee, and be saved by thee? And I heard him say, 'And him that cometh to me, I will in no wise cast out'. Then I said, But how, Lord, must I consider of thee in my coming to thee, that my faith may be placed aright upon thee? Then he said, 'Christ Jesus came into the world to save sinners'. 'He IS the end of the law for righteousness to every one that believes.' 'He died for our sins, and rose again for our justification.' 'He loved us, and washed us from our sins in his own blood.' 'He is the Mediator betwixt God and us.' 'He ever liveth to make intercession for us.'From all which I gathered, that I must look for righteousness in his person, and for satisfaction for my sins by his blood; that what he did in obedience to his Father's law, and in submitting to the penalty thereof, was not for himself, but for him that will accept it for his salvation, and be thankful. And now was my heart full of joy, mine eyes full of tears, and mine affections running over with love to the name, people, and ways of Jesus Christ.

After yesterday's readings and reflection, it should come as little surprise that in the first sentence of today's extract from *The Pilgrim's Progress* 'grace' is emphasised again, with the quotation of 2 Corinthians 12:9 and Paul's words. Paul found that God's grace was sufficient for him despite a distressing physical ailment, a 'thorn in the flesh'. Whatever it was, it was extremely difficult for Paul, but God's grace was sufficient, as it always had been. Whatever you are facing, you will find that God's grace is enough. He loves you, and that love will carry you through.

What is our response to such grace? Once again, the answer is love, but this time it's *our* love, for God and for others. Look at the final sentence of today's extract from *The Pilgrim's Progress*. With a 'heart full of joy' and 'eyes full of tears', Hopeful speaks of 'love to the name, people and ways of Jesus Christ'.

So, first of all, there is love to His name. Do we love the name of Jesus? A name speaks of someone's identity, and so this question is really another way of asking, 'do we love Jesus?' Hopeful knew he had been forgiven much, and so he loved much in return. In reality we have all been forgiven a huge debt: it has been cancelled, paid in full, 'paid on the nail' by Jesus. The more we appreciate this, the more we'll love the name of Jesus.

Do we love Christ's people? Sometimes we say we love Jesus, but we don't love the Church. This is often very understandable: churches don't always get it right. They are full of imperfect people – but we are called to love God's people. In your church, if there's a lack of love, be part of the solution, not part of the problem. Jesus has loved you and me. If He could do that for us (which He did), and if He loves us still (which He does) then our right response is to love other messed up people too!

Finally, do we love Christ's ways? Do we study to get to know His life and teaching? And as we begin to grow in understanding, do we put that knowledge into practice?

If all this seems like a tall order, it's because it is! The reality is that loving Jesus, loving others, and living for Jesus are all difficult. But God is committed to us and helps us. His commitment to us shines through again and again. Just one of the things He does is pray for us (Hebrews 7:25). Jesus is praying for you! You can keep going – because of His love for you, it is possible for you to love Him, His church and His ways. A new grace-filled life is gloriously possible because of all Jesus has done and continues to do. What amazing love!

TO PONDER ...

Love for God; love for the church; love for the ways of Jesus ...
Which one of these areas is God especially challenging you on today?

PRAYER

Father, thank You that You love me! Help me to love Your Son more, love the Church more, and follow Jesus' ways more wholeheartedly. I don't always find this easy, Lord, so I ask You to help me to live for You. Jesus, thank You that You pray for me. This fills me with inexpressible joy and confidence. Amen.

A passion for holiness

Romans 12:1; 1 Peter 1:16

Christian confirms Hopeful's testimony, but he has one last question for him. What impact has Hopeful's conversion had on his life, his ways, his thoughts and his actions? As we are about to see, the impact has been great indeed …

> *CHRISTIAN: This was a revelation of Christ to your soul indeed; but tell me particularly what effect this had upon your spirit.*
>
> *HOPEFUL: It made me see that all the world, notwithstanding all the righteousness thereof, is in a state of condemnation. It made me see that God the Father, though he be just, can justly justify the coming sinner. It made me greatly ashamed of the vileness of my former life, and confounded me with the sense of mine own ignorance; for there never came a thought into my heart before now, that showed me so the beauty of Jesus Christ. It made me love a holy life, and long to do something for the honour and glory of the name of the Lord Jesus; yea I thought, that had I now a thousand gallons of blood in my body, I could spill it all for the sake of the Lord Jesus.*

Hopeful's response to Christian's enquiry is powerful and stirring. As a result of his conversion he wants to give everything for Christ. He used to be in a 'state of condemnation', but now he is right with God; he used to be ignorant, but now he can see the 'beauty' of Jesus Christ. It is not surprising that he longs to do something for the 'honour and glory and name' of Jesus, and that his whole body is consumed by a passion for holiness.

There are two challenges for us. Firstly, there is a call to consecration, to offer ourselves completely to God. Hopeful holds nothing back. He is willing to give every last drop of blood for Jesus, living for Him and serving others out of a heart of love. Romans 12:1 challenges us in the same way – we are urged, in response to God's great 'mercy', to offer ourselves as 'living sacrifices' dedicated to God's praise and glory. Perhaps you have had such a moment of consecration in the past. The problem with living sacrifices, though, is that they have a habit of crawling off the altar! Recommit yourself, body and soul, to Jesus today.

A passion for holiness flows out of our commitment to Jesus. Holiness has a bit of a bad press. Holy people, so the thinking goes, are those who walk around with their noses in the air, spoiling all the fun – miserable killjoys who no one would want to be around. But true biblical holiness is not like that. Notice how Hopeful sees the beauty of Jesus and is led to 'love a holy life'. Holiness is Christlikeness, and Christlikeness is wonderful and deeply attractive. As we read about Jesus, as we see how He lived His life, we see holiness in action. This is the pattern for holiness the Bible commends to us, the pattern upon which Hopeful wants to model his life.

TO PONDER ...

What effect has the 'revelation of Christ' had on you?
How would you respond to Christian's question to Hopeful?

PRAYER

'Were the whole realm of nature mine,
That were an offering far too small,
Love so amazing, so divine,
Demands my soul, my life, my all.'
(Isaac Walls, 1674–1748)

Lord, thank You for giving everything for me. I want to give my all for You, depending daily on Your grace and relying on the help of the Holy Spirit. Show me where You are calling me to change. Grow in me a passion for holiness. Amen.

DAY 33

The Christian view of God

Romans 12:2

Christian and Hopeful have both been encouraged by their conversation. They carry on their journey in good heart. Soon they catch sight of Ignorance, the character they had met briefly after their escape from Doubting Castle. At that time they had decided he was not ready for a spiritual conversation, but now they perceive that he is. They wait for him to catch up with them.

Christian is quite direct with Ignorance, immediately asking him 'how stands it between God and your soul now?' Ignorance doesn't seem to mind the question and responds positively. He explains to Christian that he has a good heart and leads a good life and therefore his 'hope is well grounded'. Christian sees the fatal flaw in Ignorance's understanding and so continues to question him. But Ignorance is, as his name suggests, ignorant of the gospel truth and does not understand salvation through grace. He asks Christian for clarification.

IGNORANCE: What are good thoughts concerning God?

CHRISTIAN: Even as I have said concerning ourselves, when our thoughts of God do agree with what the Word saith of him; and that is, when we think of his being and attributes as the Word hath taught, of which I cannot now discourse at large; but to speak of him with reference to us: Then have we right thoughts of God, when we think that he knows us better than we know ourselves, and can see sin in us when and where we can see none in ourselves; when we think he knows our inmost thoughts, and that our heart, with all its depths, is always open unto his eyes;

also when we think that all our righteousness stinks in his nostrils, and that, therefore, he cannot abide to see us stand before him in any confidence, even in all our best performances.

Ignorance is mistaken in his view of God and of himself – he cannot believe that his heart is 'bad' and he understands very little about the character of God. Christian tries to put him right, and his words reveal a deep knowledge of both the human condition and the one, true God. How does Christian know the truth? Is it because he is cleverer than Ignorance? This is not the case – in fact, we have seen Christian going his own way at different times in the story and making some very foolish mistakes. No, Christian is able to speak so clearly and helpfully because he bases what he says on God's Word, the Bible, which is trustworthy and true.

Yesterday we looked at Romans 12:1 and the call to give ourselves wholly to God. Romans 12:2 encourages us not to be conformed 'to the pattern of this world'. Rather, we are to be 'transformed by the renewing of our minds'. This happens when we bring our thinking into line with God's thinking, as revealed in His Word.

This is a wonderful challenge but it is not an easy one. It is much easier to let 'the world squeeze you into its mould', as J.B. Phillips once interpreted this verse. To be shaped by God's Word takes discipline – we need to take the time to read and meditate on it. It takes prayer, for we need the power of the Holy Spirit to understand it and see how it applies to us. And it takes Spirit-inspired courage if we are going to stand out from the crowd and live gracious, light-filled, Word-shaped lives for Jesus. Ignorance wasn't up for the challenge. Are we?

TO PONDER ...

Take some time to reflect prayerfully on your life. Are there areas where you sense you are being transformed by the Spirit as you read God's Word? Give thanks to God, and pray that He would take you deeper, in both understanding and action.

Are there areas where you sense the world is 'squeezing you into its mould', perhaps in your attitudes to money, power, or relationships? Be open to hearing God's voice. Note down where you sense God is challenging you.

PRAYER

Lord, thank You that Your Word reveals the truth about You, and about who I am in You. Help me to be shaped by Your Word every day, in my thinking, speaking and acting. I pray for the courage and strength to be different. Thank You for challenging me today, and for giving me the power to change by Your Spirit. Amen.

Ignorance or understanding?

Mark 14:66–72

Despite Christian and Hopeful talking with him, it is clear that Ignorance is blind to the message of the gospel. He has no real sense of his own sinfulness, so how can he understand his need for a Saviour? Christian and Hopeful are very concerned for his soul and try their best to explain the meaning of true faith in Christ, but Ignorance remains stubbornly ignorant. He does not want to hear of justification through Christ or talk of 'revelations', calling these 'the fruit of distracted brains'. His faith, he says to them, is as good as theirs. Christian, desperate not to leave him in 'ignorance', entreats him one last time to look to Christ and be saved.

CHRISTIAN: Give me leave to put in a word. You ought not so slightly to speak of this matter; for this I will boldly affirm, even as my good companion hath done, that no man can know Jesus Christ but by the revelation of the Father, yea, and faith too, by which the soul layeth hold upon Christ, if it be right, must be wrought by the exceeding greatness of his mighty power; the working of which faith, I perceive, poor Ignorance, thou art ignorant of. Be awakened then, see thine own wretchedness, and fly to the Lord Jesus; and by his righteousness, which is the righteousness of God, for he himself is God, thou shalt be delivered from condemnation.

IGNORANCE: You go so fast, I cannot keep pace with you. Do you go on before; I must stay a while behind.

There is some irony in the reading from *The Pilgrim's Progress* today, when Christian tells Ignorance he is 'ignorant'. This may seem humorous, but of course the reality is deadly serious. Ignorance cannot keep up in the pilgrimage. The truth about God and about himself is too much for him.

We are all 'ignorant' sometimes. We misunderstand, we say the wrong thing, we let God down. The apostle Peter is a great example of this. He told Jesus he wasn't going to suffer (Mark 8:32–33), and denied Jesus three times (our reading for today, Mark 14:66–72). And even after he had received the Spirit at Pentecost he was still prone to failure, saying 'Surely not, Lord!' when God revealed His truth to Him (Acts 10:14) and when he refused to eat with Gentiles (Galatians 2:11). God persevered with him, which is great encouragement to us. But still we should pause, reflect and pray. When have we been ignorant, and let God down? Pray today for God's forgiveness, and for wisdom – and strength – to be different in the future.

There is a deeper type of ignorance though, a stubbornness and hardness of heart. This is the ignorance that Bunyan is really portraying here. The story of 'Ignorance' is a tragic one.

There is real sadness as Ignorance wearily gasps, 'You go so fast, I cannot keep pace with you' and tells Christian and Hopeful to press ahead without him. Today, pray for a real breakthrough in the lives of people you know, people who may be hardened, confused, or weary (or maybe all three). God is able to do more than we 'ask or imagine' (Ephesians 3:20).

TO PONDER ...

On day two you prayed for three people. How are they doing? Are you still praying for them? Whatever their situation, thank God for them and continue to pray for God to work in their lives.

PRAYER

Lord, help me to grow and live in knowledge and understanding of Your character and Your ways. Forgive me for the times I have been 'ignorant', either wilfully or by mistake. Thank You that You love me and give me a fresh start. Amen.

And all the trumpets sounded for him on the other side

'Life, life, eternal life'

IN COMMEMORATION OF THE TERCENTENARY OF THE DEATH
· OF JOHN BUNYAN 1688—1988 ·

In remembrance of Frederick Shreeves 1858-1938 and his family placed here by a grandson

The glory and the wonder

Mark 9:2–13; Isaiah 62

Christian and Hopeful continue on their way together, with Ignorance hobbling after. They are both saddened that Ignorance will most likely not make it to the Celestial City.

The two pilgrims have proved to be great travelling companions, both enjoying the company of the other and being inspired by the depth of spiritual conversation. They are now nearing the end of their earthly pilgrimage. To give them renewed strength and hope for the final part of their journey, the pilgrims enjoy a time of peace and tranquillity in a beautiful land on the 'borders of heaven'.

Now I saw in my dream, that by this time the Pilgrims were got over the Enchanted Ground, and entering into the country of Beulah, whose air was very sweet and pleasant, the way lying directly through it, they solaced themselves there for a season. Yea, here they heard continually the singing of birds, and saw every day the flowers appear in the earth, and heard the voice of the turtle in the land. In this country the sun shineth night and day; wherefore this was beyond the Valley of the Shadow of Death, and also out of the reach of Giant Despair, neither could they from this place so much as see Doubting Castle. Here they were within sight of the city they were going to: also here met them some of the inhabitants thereof; for in this land the Shining Ones commonly walked, because it was upon the borders of heaven. In this land also the contract between the bride and the bridegroom was renewed; yea here, 'As the bridegroom rejoiceth over the bride, so did their God rejoice over them'. Here they had no want of corn and wine; for in this place they met with abundance of what they had sought for in all their pilgrimage. Here they heard voices from out of the city, loud voices, saying, 'Say ye to the daughter of Zion, Behold, thy salvation cometh! Behold, his reward IS with him.'

In the Bible the name 'Beulah' signifies a land that is blessed by God and that is 'married' to Him (Isaiah 62:4). Christian and Hopeful have entered into that land 'for a season' – this is not their final destination. The Celestial City still awaits them; there is more to come! Yet they have reached a place where heaven touches earth. The powers of the age to come are breaking through in significant ways. And it is wonderful.

Bunyan describes this land beautifully. There is 'heavenly' companionship. Doubting Castle and Giant Despair are distant memories. The pilgrims' journey has been overshadowed by darkness on a number of occasions, but here the light shines brightly 'night and day'. There are new flowers every morning and the air smells sweet. Mentioning the 'voice of the turtle' seems strange. What would that sound like?! But for seventeenth-century readers this would have seemed exotic, as if it came from a story about paradise. Sights and sounds and smells combine to present a glorious picture full of superabundant life and colour. The land is so beautiful because God is there.

The passage reminds us that our Christian pilgrimage leads somewhere wonderful and glorious, as Beulah is a foretaste of heaven. If you are overshadowed by darkness at the moment keep going, because the time is coming when the light will break through and the darkness will be gone.

But God gives us so much here and now, too. Bunyan's pilgrims experienced God's closeness while they were still on their journey, and Peter, James and John experienced the transfiguration of Jesus whilst they were still earthly disciples, in the midst of all the pressures of life and ministry. For them the curtain was pulled back, just for a moment. They saw Jesus in all His brilliant, blazing brightness. They saw His glory; they beheld His splendour.

We may not have Beulah or transfiguration experiences (and these don't tend to be everyday occurrences in the Christian life!), but as we press on to know God more He does reveal Himself to us. We taste heavenly realities. We learn to delight in Him, and increasingly we realise how amazing God is. So pursue God! Search after Him. And may God reveal Himself to you, in His power and His love.

TO PONDER ...

Spend some more time reflecting on the picture of 'Beulah'. What is it about the description you find most attractive? Resolve to press on to know God more and find your joy in Him.

PRAYER

Lord, thank You that You are the all-glorious God! Help me to pursue You with a passion. Thank You that, because of Your grace, You reward those who seek You. Lead me forward, Jesus. I will follow. Amen.

Fear not

Isaiah 43:1–3

There are just two more hurdles that Christian and Hopeful must overcome before they can come face to face with Christ their Lord. The first of the two is the most terrible: the river of death.

Two angels have come to greet the pilgrims and to offer encouragement. They promise to accompany the pilgrims across the river but, they tell them, they cannot help them – Christian and Hopeful must cross in the strength of their own faith. Only two men have ever escaped such a river – Enoch and Elijah – and that was by the special command of God. The pilgrims enquire of the angels whether the waters are all of the same depth. 'No,' reply the angels, 'You shall find it deeper or shallower, as you believe in the King of the place.'

Christian and Hopeful enter the river. Perhaps surprisingly, given that he is the older pilgrim, it is Christian who struggles the most and who needs to draw upon the strength of his younger and more 'Hopeful' companion to help him across.

> *Hopeful, therefore, here had much ado to keep his brother's head above water; yea, sometimes he would be quite gone down, and then, ere a while, he would rise up again half dead. Hopeful also would endeavour to comfort him, saying, Brother, I see the gate, and men standing by to receive us; but Christian would answer, It is you, it is you they wait for; you have been Hopeful ever since I knew you. And so have you, said he to Christian. Ah, brother! said he, surely if I was right he would now arise to help me; but for my sins he hath brought me into the snare, and hath left me.*

Then said Hopeful, My brother, you have quite forgot the text, where it is said of the wicked, THERE ARE no bands in their death; but their strength IS firm, they ARE not in trouble AS OTHER men, neither are they plagued like OTHER men. These troubles and distresses that you go through in these waters, are no sign that God hath forsaken you; but are sent to try you, whether you will call to mind that which heretofore you have received of his goodness, and live upon him in your distresses.

Then I saw in my dream that Christian was as in a muse a while. To whom also Hopeful added this word, Be of good cheer, Jesus Christ maketh thee whole; and with that Christian brake out with a loud voice, O! I see him again, and he tells me, 'When thou passest through the waters, I WILL BE with thee; and through the rivers, they shall not overflow thee.' Then they both took courage, and the enemy was after that as still as a stone, until they were gone over. Christian therefore presently found ground to stand upon, and so it followed that the rest of the river was but shallow. Thus they got over.

Death – the final enemy. The 'river' that Christian and Hopeful cross is one that we will all have to face. As Bunyan reminds us, there is no way by which we might escape it. But for the Christian, even death will be defeated. On the other side of the river there is a more glorious future for all who have truly trusted in Christ as their Saviour.

Yet, as this passage demonstrates, a secure faith is no guarantee of an easy crossing. Even mature Christians can find their faith tested and challenged at the point of death. As the two pilgrims wade into the river, it is Christian, the elder of the two, who is suddenly wracked with doubts and finds himself sinking. Bunyan tells us that 'a great darkness and horror fell upon Christian'; that 'he was much in the troublesome thoughts of the sins that he had committed, both since and before he began to be a pilgrim' and that he even doubted his salvation. Such are the terrors that overcome Christian as he enters the river.

But thankfully, Christian is not alone. He has his 'Hopeful' companion with him. Hopeful is able to help him, at times by managing to keep his head above water, at other times with words of comfort and encouragement. He speaks with spiritual maturity as he assures Christian that his struggles are actually a sign of true faith; struggles actually sent to try him, to see whether he will recall God's goodness to him on his journey and call upon God again in his distress. He then encourages Christian to look to Christ. Christian's hope returns and from that point on, we are told; the river is 'but shallow'. Once again, Bunyan shows us the importance of Christian companionship. Christian crosses the river in his own faith, but having a 'Hopeful' companion has made the crossing easier. As Christians, we are called to be companions both in life and in death.

Whatever our circumstances when we come to cross that river, there is one companion who will always be with us and who will help us as we cross, just as he helped Christian when he looked to Him. It is Jesus Christ – 'the Alpha and Omega' (Revelation 1:8) – the beginning and the end. God's promises to those that trust in Him are real promises. Look again at today's reading and focus on the promises it contains: 'Fear not'; 'I will be with you'; 'when you pass through the rivers, they will not sweep over you'. Death will never be easy. There will be a 'river' to cross. But, as Christian and Hopeful found, it will be 'deeper or shallower' according to the trust we place in God. In death, as in life, God's promises stand firm. It is for us to call upon them.

TO PONDER ...

'For me be it Christ, be it Christ hence to live!
If Jordan above me shall roll,
No pang shall be mine, for in death as in life
Thou wilt whisper Thy peace to my soul.'
(Horatio Gates Spafford, 1828–1888)

PRAYER

Father, I thank You for all of Your promises. Today, help me rest assured in Your promise that 'For me to live is Christ, and to die is gain'. Jesus, You are hope, You are joy, You are life. Amen.

A new heaven and a new earth

Revelation 21:1–7

The pilgrims are across! The river of death has been defeated and they have reached the other side.

Here they are greeted by the same two angels who were watching over them as they crossed. Christian and Hopeful must now climb the hill that leads to the heavenly city. This is their final hurdle but, we are told, they do this 'with ease' for they have left their earthly garments in the river and have angels – 'such glorious companions' – to help them. As they ascend the hill, the angels encourage them with talk of the 'inexpressible' beauty and glory of heaven.

The men then asked, What must we do in the holy place? To whom it was answered, You must there receive the comfort of all your toil, and have joy for all your sorrow; you must reap what you have sown, even the fruit of all your prayers, and tears, and sufferings for the King by the way. In that place you must wear crowns of gold, and enjoy the perpetual sight and vision of the Holy One, for 'there you shall see him as he is'. There also you shall serve him continually with praise, with shouting and thanksgiving, whom you desired to serve in the world, though with much difficulty, because of the infirmity of your flesh. There your eyes shall be delighted with seeing, and your ears with hearing the pleasant voice of the Mighty One. There you shall enjoy your friends again, that are gone thither before you; and there you shall with joy receive, even every one that follows into the holy place after you. There also you

shall be clothed with glory and majesty, and put into an equipage
fit to ride out with the King of glory. When he shall come with
sound of trumpet in the clouds, as upon the wings of the wind,
you shall come with him; and when he shall sit upon the throne of
judgment, you shall sit by him; yea, and when he shall pass sentence
upon all the workers of iniquity, let them be angels or men, you
also shall have a voice in that judgment, because they were his and
your enemies. Also when he shall again return to the city, you shall
go too, with sound of trumpet, and be ever with him.

The Celestial City is in sight. Christian and Hopeful's earthly challenges are finally over and they can look forward to a wonderful reception in heaven. They have their scrolls with them, certificates that assure them of their entrance into the Celestial City and an eternity with Christ their Saviour. As the pilgrims ascend the hill, the angels accompanying them tell them what to expect, and it is a glorious account. So many beautiful words! So many promises! After such a perilous journey, this must truly be music to the tired pilgrims' ears.

We need more of this 'music' to encourage us as we travel on. Bunyan's allegory actually starts with a statement telling us that Christian *will* arrive at the Celestial City. We know at the outset what his destination is and that he will reach it. Bunyan wants us to be encouraged by this, for it is an assurance that all true believers share. He wants our own 'safe arrival at the desired country' to be as much a focus for us on our journey as it was for Christian and his companions. Bunyan wants to remind us of the absolute beauty and wonder of this final destination and to encourage us to keep our eyes fixed on the prize ahead of us. So, right at the beginning we have a reminder and a promise of our destination; and at the end, some beautifully descriptive passages of the 'inexpressible' beauty and glory of heaven.

Dwell on today's passages from Revelation and *The Pilgrim's Progress* for a few moments. Read them again slowly. Consider the language Bunyan uses to describe the Celestial City. The angels promise true pilgrims 'comfort of all your toil', 'joy for all your sorrow', and 'the fruit of all your prayers and tears'. Pilgrims will 'wear crowns of gold' and 'enjoy perpetual sight and visions of the holy one'. We are promised that there we shall 'enjoy' our friends again who have gone there before us; and we shall 'with joy' receive those that follow after. We will be 'clothed with glory and majesty' and serve God 'continually with praise'. This sounds amazing! Yet this is still a poor and inadequate description of a Celestial City whose real beauty and glory is 'inexpressible'. The Celestial City that we are journeying towards is even more beautiful, even more glorious than the words here can describe, and it is God's ultimate promise to all who truly believe. Like Christian, we too are promised our 'safe arrival at the desired country'. Like Christian, we too should keep our eyes fixed on this most wonderful of destinations.

TO PONDER ...

'Finish then Thy new creation,
Pure and spotless let us be;
Let us see Thy great salvation,
Perfectly restored in Thee;
Changed from glory into glory,
Till in heaven we take our place,
Till we cast our crowns before Thee,
Lost in wonder, love and praise.'
(Charles Wesley, 1707–1788)

PRAYER

Father, thank You that in Your house there are many 'mansions', and that there is a place there for even me. Thank You for the hope that this gives me in life, and for the comfort in death. In all of the wonders of life here on earth, help me to keep my eyes fixed on the glory of heaven. Amen.

Life, life, eternal life

Revelation 22:1–7

Christian and Hopeful are almost inside the gate. As they draw near, they are greeted by 'a company of the heavenly host'. The two angels that have accompanied them thus far explain that these are pilgrims that have loved and followed Christ and are now ready to meet their Saviour. At this there is much rejoicing. Trumpets are sounded and the pilgrims given such a welcome that it was 'as if heaven itself was come down to meet them'. Angels surround them with joyful music – celebrations that continue all the way up to the gate of heaven. Here the pilgrims are greeted by Enoch, Moses and Elijah. Christian and Hopeful hand over their certificates to them and wait while they are read by the King. Then the long-awaited moment arrives. The King commands that the gate be opened. It is time for Christian and Hopeful to enter the Celestial City and receive their reward, the promised 'Life, Life, Eternal Life'.

Now I saw in my dream that these two men went in at the gate; and lo, as they entered, they were transfigured, and they had raiment put on that shone like gold. There was also that met them with harps and crowns, and gave them to them - the harps to praise withal, and the crowns in token of honour. Then I heard in my dream that all the bells in the city rang again for joy; and that it was said unto them, 'ENTER YE INTO THE JOY OF YOUR LORD'. I also heard the men themselves, that they sang with a loud voice, saying, 'BLESSING, AND HONOUR, AND GLORY, AND POWER, BE UNTO HIM THAT SITTETH UPON THE THRONE, AND UNTO THE LAMB, FOR EVER AND EVER.'

Now just as the gates were opened to let in the men, I looked in after them, and behold, the City shone like the sun; the streets also were paved with gold, and in them walked many men, with crowns on their heads, palms in their hands, and golden harps to sing praises withal.

There were also of them that had wings, and they answered one another without intermission, saying, 'Holy, Holy, Holy is the Lord'. And after that, they shut up the gates: which, when I had seen, I wished myself among them.

When Christian first met Evangelist at the start of the story, he wanted to know what he had to do to be 'saved'. Christian's reading of the Bible – the 'book' – had not only warned him of the 'grave', it had given him the hope of salvation. Evangelist's initial role was to point Christian in the right direction, towards the 'light'. And Christian responded. Ignoring the pleas of his wife and children, he 'put his fingers in his ears, and ran on' crying out, 'Life, Life, Eternal Life'. The promise of eternal life was more important to Christian than anything, even his wife and children.

And now he has arrived! At last, after many 'dangers, toils and snares', Christian has reached his final destination. His salvation is realised. He is safely home and 'Life, life, eternal life' is now his. What a moment! There is music, there is joy, there is singing; there are new clothes and golden crowns; and there is light. So much light! Bunyan tells us that the city 'shone like the sun'; Revelation teaches that 'they will not need the light of a lamp or the light of the sun, for the Lord God will give them light'. Just as Christ is the light that we need on earth, so Christ is all the light that we will need in heaven. Christian had run to the wicket gate and found the light that was to guide him on his earthly pilgrimage. Now he has entered the gates of heaven and is encompassed by eternal light. It is a light that will never go out – God's ultimate promise to us, His children.

We should take time to reflect on this promise. Yesterday we took a few moments to reflect on Bunyan's words as he described the promise of heaven that awaited the faithful pilgrims. Today, let us reflect on our Scripture reading, the passage from Revelation. The words and the promises contained within this passage are so wonderful that they deserve more than a quick reading. Take time. Dwell on each sentence. Let the imagery flood your mind and fill you with wonder. This is heaven! This is our destination! One day we will see for ourselves 'the river of the water of life, as clear as crystal, flowing from the throne of God and of the Lamb'. We will see the tree of life with leaves 'for the healing of the nations'. We will bask in eternal light, we will see the face of the Lamb and we will reign with Him for ever and ever. What a promise!

Keep that image in your mind as you go back to today's text from Bunyan's story and read again the final sentence. It is a powerful one, surely designed to make us think. The dreamer has been allowed a glimpse of heaven, a taste of the glory to come. It is a glimpse that makes him want more: 'which when I had seen, I wished myself among them'. The gates are shut and the dreamer can no longer see in but the impact has been powerful. Life on earth, even with the best of its God-given pleasures, attractions and opportunities, has no hold on him now; his desire is for the beauty, the wonder, the glory of heaven. How much more should it be ours too.

TO PONDER ...

Bunyan was a man who really knew his Bible – as was C.S. Lewis, who allegedly would memorise a chapter of the Bible each day! This is not a skill that is taught or used much today, but perhaps it should be. As Christians, committing key scriptures to memory must surely be a worthwhile task.

So today, spend a few moments committing some of today's Bible passage to memory. You may wish to focus on just a sentence or two, or you may want to challenge yourself to learning the whole passage. It is a beautiful passage and full of the Christian hope. Keep it close to your heart. You never know when you might need it.

PRAYER

Father, today I want to give You thanks for the promise of eternal life. Thank You for loving the world, and for loving me, so much that You sent Jesus to earth to die for us. And thank You for leaving us Your Word. Help me to know it more deeply and through it to understand more of You and Your love for me. Amen.

Awakening and converting work

Luke 13:22–30

Bunyan ends his story with a shocking conclusion. After the wonderfully vivid and glorious descriptions of heaven and the celebrations that accompany Christian and Hopeful's safe arrival, this is not what the reader expects. It is quite horrific. For Bunyan, hell was – and is – real. His heart was for 'awakening and converting work'. He desperately wanted to see men and women saved from an eternity without God. So his ending is not a description of the joys of heaven; rather it is a shocking reminder of the reality of hell.

Now while I was gazing upon all these things, I turned my head to look back, and saw Ignorance come up to the river side; but he soon got over, and that without half the difficulty which the other two men met with. For it happened, that there was then in that place one Vain-hope, a ferryman, that with his boat helped him over; so he, as the other I saw, did ascend the hill, to come up to the gate, only he came alone; neither did any man meet him with the least encouragement. When he was come up to the gate, he looked up to the writing that was above; and then began to knock, supposing that entrance should have been quickly administered to him; but he was asked by the men that looked over the top of the gate, Whence came you? and what would you have? He answered, I have eat and drank in the presence of the King, and he has taught in our streets. Then they asked him for his certificate, that they might go in and show it to the King; so he fumbled in his bosom for one, and found none. Then said they, Have you none? But the man answered never a word. So they told the King, but he would not come down to see him, but commanded the two Shining Ones that conducted Christian and Hopeful to the City, to go out and take Ignorance, and bind him hand and foot, and have him away. Then they took him up, and carried him through the air to the door that I saw in the side of the hill, and put him in there. Then I saw that there was a way to hell, even from the gates of heaven, as well as from the City of Destruction! So I awoke, and behold it was a dream.

What a way to end the book! How do we respond? Do we recoil from Bunyan concluding his book in this way? How can the glorious testimony to the immeasurable grace of God that is *The Pilgrim's Progress* end in this way? We can recoil from the very thought of hell. Is there such a place? Surely not! Or we might read with fear and trembling. If we have a heart we might well weep for Ignorance as he fumbles in vain for his 'certificate'. If we have God's heart we will certainly weep for him.

This may not be a pleasant way for *The Pilgrim's Progress* to conclude, but nevertheless, it is important. Bunyan didn't want to give false hope. Part of his intention was to awaken his audience to the terrible reality of an eternity without God. He did this because he was clear that this was the fate of all who refuse to come to God in faith and receive His salvation; and because he knew the teaching of Jesus, in passages like our reading today from Luke 13. It is not loving to pretend that hell doesn't exist. Those like Vain-hope did that. The loving thing to do would have been to warn Ignorance, to urge him to get right with God. But Vain-hope failed. And then it was too late.

The end of Bunyan's story challenges our culture and the culture of many of our churches. It challenges us. Have we sometimes given 'vain-hope' to someone? It is not loving to give false hope. Those who are trying to get to God by some other pathway, such as good works or churchgoing, need to come to Jesus. So the challenge is to renew our commitment to what Bunyan calls 'awakening and converting work'. Of course, it is God who does the awakening, and the converting too. But he uses us. Firstly, He uses our prayers. Keep bringing before Him friends and neighbours, relatives and work colleagues. God is gracious and He responds to our prayers and turns 'ignorant' hearts to Him. Secondly, He uses our lives. When we are full of love, speaking both grace and truth, we reflect the life of Jesus our Lord, who was – and is – the 'friend of sinners' (Matthew 11:19). Thirdly and finally, He calls us to speak. So, pray, live and tell the gospel today. This was Bunyan's passion, his only desired legacy. Let's make it ours too.

TO PONDER …

Pray, live and tell the gospel. Which of these three challenges is sharpest for us? Maybe we pray much but never speak about Jesus? Or perhaps we speak about Him, but as we reflect we recognise that our life doesn't always back up what we say. As you come to God in prayer, ask for forgiveness, and for the strength and power to be a clearer witness for Jesus.

PRAYER

Lord, thank You for inviting me to join in Your wonderful work of turning people from darkness to light. Show me those You are calling me to pray for, and give me opportunities to speak for You. Most of all, help me to live a life that reflects the character of Jesus. Thank You, once again, for Your grace to me. Help me now to share that grace with others. Amen.

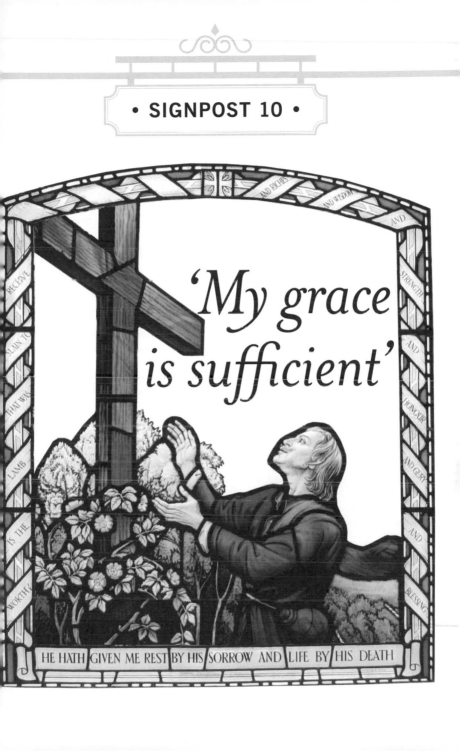

'My grace is sufficient'

HE HATH GIVEN ME REST BY HIS SORROW AND LIFE BY HIS DEATH

Preserving the gold

2 Timothy 1:13–14

We have reached the end of our journey. The pilgrim, Christian, has reached his destination. 'Life, life, eternal life!' is now his to enjoy forever. With him are his 'Faithful' and 'Hopeful' companions. They have all now entered into 'the joy of the Lord', a joy so beautiful that Bunyan is compelled to reflect, 'I wished myself among them', as the gates to heaven close behind the blessed pilgrims.

But Bunyan has not quite finished! In his conclusion, he has one last thing to say to us, his readers. He asks us to 'preserve the gold'. The message of the book is not to be discarded and forgotten; rather, 'the substance' of it should be treasured and preserved. As yesterday's reflection reminds us, the message his story conveys is a vital one. It is not to be ignored.

Now, READER, I have told my dream to thee;
See if thou canst interpret it to me,
Or to thyself, or neighbour; but take heed
Of misinterpreting; for that, instead
Of doing good, will but thyself abuse:
By misinterpreting, evil ensues …

… What of my dross thou findest there, be bold
To throw away, but yet preserve the gold;
What if my gold be wrapped up in ore?
None throws away the apple for the core.
But if thou shalt cast all away as vain,
I know not but 'twill make me dream again.

What of his 'dream' will you preserve? There is so much! There are scenes that surely will never leave us: Christian with his 'great burden', crying out 'what shall I do?'; Evangelist pointing the way; Worldly-wiseman; Christian at the wicket gate; the house of the Interpreter; Christian at the cross; Hill Difficulty and the palace Beautiful; the fight with Apollyon; the death of Faithful at Vanity Fair; the conversations with Talkative and Ignorance; Doubting Castle; the country of Beulah on the borders of heaven; the river of death; the Celestial City. And many, many more ...

Then there are simple phrases that stand out, showing Bunyan's immense spiritual knowledge, wisdom and passion: 'God with reference to us' compels us to understand human sinfulness in relation to an almighty God; 'and I saw it no more' assures Christians their burden of sin has been dealt with once and for all at the cross of Christ; 'as God would have it' and 'he that over-rules all things' speak of God's sovereignty; and 'life, life, eternal life' reminds us of the abundant life God gives all Christian pilgrims – life now and life in the age to come.

Finally, there is an abundance of biblical references. Bunyan's faith was rooted in the Scriptures and he wants ours to be too. Every character, every symbol, every message he conveys through his story has its foundation in God's Word. And while every lesson within *The Pilgrim's Progress* is important, it is the good news of the gospel, summed up in the following key verses, that inspired and drove Bunyan: 'Knock and it shall be opened unto you'; 'my grace is sufficient for you'; 'in all these things we are more than conquerors, through him that loved us'; and 'behold thy salvation cometh!'

But we leave you with what is possibly the most beautiful passage to be found in *The Pilgrim's Progress*. It comes from the scene at the cross, the moment when Christian loses his 'great burden'. Take a moment to imagine yourself in Christian's place. You too are standing at the foot of the cross. You have a vision of Christ crucified, an undeserving sacrifice. All your sin, your guilt, your shame has been lifted from you. Christ has given you 'rest by his sorrow; and life by his death'. One day you too will receive the crown of life. Like Christian, your eyes well up with 'springs' of healing tears and your heart overflows with joy. Christ died for you, even you. Such love! Such amazing grace!

Thus far did I come laden with my sin,
Nor could ought ease the grief that I was in,
Till I came hither: What a place is this!
Must here be the beginning of my bliss?
Must here the burden fall from off my back?
Must here the strings that bound it to me, crack?
Blest cross! Blest sepulchre! Blest rather be
The man that there was put to shame for me.

TO PONDER ...

'Then you will know the truth, and the truth will set you free'
(John 8:32).

PRAYER

Thank You, Father, for sending Your Son into this world. Thank You that Your love for me is so great that He died on the cross so that I might have 'life, life, eternal life'. Thank You for what I've read and explored over the last forty days. Help me daily to be a living sacrifice as I continue to live every day of my life for You. Amen.

Follow the footsteps of a pilgrim

JOHN BUNYAN: THE PEOPLE'S PILGRIM DVD

The inspiring life story of John Bunyan comes alive in this new docudrama DVD, produced by CTA. Watch it unfold as the bold evangelist, who was imprisoned for preaching the gospel, faces the challenges and triumphs of life.

EAN: 5027957-001657

JOHN BUNYAN: THE PEOPLE'S PILGRIM BOOK

A lively and engaging account of the life of *The Pilgrim's Progress* author, John Bunyan. In this full-colour, beautifully illustrated book, Peter Morden blends historical context as well as fresh insight into this historic man of God.

ISBN: 978-1-85354-836-1

Also available as an interactive PDF.

For current prices and to order, visit **www.cwr.org.uk/store** or call **01252 784700.**
Also available in Christian bookshops.

Continue transforming your daily walk with God

Subscribe or try out an issue of one of CWR's Bible reading notes. Choose the perfect one for you and continue to explore the Bible and your relationship with God, every day.

EVERY DAY WITH JESUS

This trusted devotional, read by over half a million people, gleans from the 40 years of Selwyn Hughes' renowned writing and is updated by Mick Brooks.

LIFE EVERY DAY

Well-known speaker and author Jeff Lucas helps make the Bible relevant to life each day through his trademark passion, humour and insight.

INSPIRING WOMEN EVERY DAY

Written by women for women, each day of this award winning devotional provides inspiration, insight, challenge and encouragement.

COVER TO COVER EVERY DAY

Respected Bible teachers explore one Old and one New Testament book in each issue. This in-depth Bible reading devotional covers the entire Bible in five years.

For current prices and to order or subscribe, visit **www.cwr.org.uk/store** or call **01252 784700**. Also available in Christian bookshops.

 Printed subscription available Large print subscription available Email subscription available

Courses and events

Waverley Abbey College

Publishing and media

Conference facilities

Transforming lives

CWR's vision is to enable people to experience personal transformation through applying God's Word to their lives and relationships.

Our Bible-based training and resources help people around the world to:
• Grow in their walk with God
• Understand and apply Scripture to their lives
• Resource themselves and their church
• Develop pastoral care and counselling skills
• Train for leadership
• Strengthen relationships, marriage and family life and much more.

CWR Applying God's Word
to everyday life and relationships

CWR, Waverley Abbey House,
Waverley Lane, Farnham,
Surrey GU9 8EP, UK

Telephone: +44 (0)1252 784700
Email: info@cwr.org.uk
Website: www.cwr.org.uk

Registered Charity No. 294387
Company Registration No. 1990308

Our insightful writers provide daily Bible-reading notes and other resources for all ages, and our experienced course designers and presenters have gained an international reputation for excellence and effectiveness.

CWR's Training and Conference Centres in Surrey and East Sussex, England, provide excellent facilities in idyllic settings – ideal for both learning and spiritual refreshment.